vintage muggeridge

religion and society

malcolm muggeridge

(ed.) GEOFFREY BARLOW

Angel Press

Publishers

First published by Angel Press,
PO Box 60, Chichester, West Sussex
in 1985

The publishers acknowledge with thanks the assistance of the following: William F. Buckley, Jr; J.P. McFadden of *The Human Life Review;* Pro Fide Forum; Christianity Today; *Toronto Globe and Mail;* The Saint Andrew Press; The Bible Society, Australia; St Ignatius Institute; University of San Francisco; *The Tablet* and *New Statesman,* and Harper and Row Inc.

Cover photograph by Francis Proctor

British Library Cataloguing in Publication Data
Muggeridge, Malcolm
Vintage Muggeridge : religion and society
1. Muggeridge, Malcolm 2. Christianity
I. Title II. Barlow, Geoffrey
209'.2'4 BR121.2

ISBN 0-94778-507-8

Produced by Arachne Marketing Services
and printed in England by
Conifer Press

Contents

Editor's Preface

Nothing has given me more pleasure than preparing and editing this book – 'Vintage Muggeridge'.

To have researched the various lectures and addresses that have been delivered over the years by Malcolm was certainly quite an experience. They are as fresh and applicable to us all to-day, as many of them were when written several years ago.

I would like to thank Elizabeth Longford, Lord Coggan, Richard Ingrams, Robert Emmett Tyrrell, Jr, and Bishop Cormac Murphy-O'Connor of Arundel and Brighton for their contributions to the book, Malcolm and Kitty Muggeridge for their help and advice, my wife Naomi for all her encouragement, and Jane Soane for typing all the manuscripts, and all the co-operation and assistance I have had from the publishers of this book, 'Angel Press'.

Geoffrey Barlow, Sussex 1985

Introduction

It was the happiest of days for me and my family when Malcolm and Kitty came back to live in Sussex. They returned as travellers who knew much of the world: Egypt, India, Russia, North America. Gradually I came to realise that Malcolm was also a traveller who had returned from one of the buffer states between the barren wastes of scepticism and the green land of Christendom. His deepest wish is to guide others into those 'green pastures' where he himself now lives.

He has always distrusted the manufacture of laughter for its own sake – he was uneasy as the editor of *Punch* – and today he uses his great gifts of irony, wit and style in the cause of humanity itself. In that sense he is indeed a guru, a 'Saint Mugg' jeered at by unbelievers, many of whom stay to praise.

I remember Kitty once telling me about a young man who arrived in Sussex from Canada with nothing but his rucksack. The Muggeridges returned from a lecture to find him on their doorstep. "I'm here," was all he said. Kitty looked after him for a week so that he could sit at Malcolm's feet.

Malcolm does not believe in political placebos, though of course he recognises the need for government. He turns naturally to Christ's words: "Render unto Caesar the things that are Caesar's and to God the things that are

God's." His special mission is to stop Caesar from making away with the lot.

Setting apart the teaching of Jesus, from which he and Kitty read aloud every day, I would say that a line from the poetry of William Blake is the source of his vision and explains his line of attack on materialism. Blake wrote that, "You" – you and I and all of us – "believe a Lie / When you see with, not thro', the eye." In Blake's mind there seems to be a double meaning attached to his wish that we should see *through* our eyes rather than *with* them. According to the first sense, we are no longer deceived by our eyes; we 'see through' their deceptions. But, equally important, we can learn to 'see through' our eyes, as if with miraculous lenses, to the truth behind the surface impression. When Malcolm saw Mother Teresa holding up a tiny living baby she had rescued from a dustbin, he discovered that he was really seeing "another 'Lamb of God' sent into the world to lighten our darkness."

This collection of vintage (non-alcoholic!) Muggeridge is a boon to us all. It will bring Malcolm vividly before those who have heard him speak and who want to cheer and fortify themselves by reading him at will.

Elizabeth Longford

Am I a Christian?

The subject that has been chosen tonight is one that to me is of immense seriousness. Am I a Christian? I don't think it's merely of seriousness to me. I think that many people who might in their normal habits of thought and ways seem very remote from any connection with the Christian religion might well be putting that question and putting it sometimes with great disconcertment. Am I a Christian? It ought to be the easiest question in the world to answer. A Christian is a follower of Christ, and I'm quite sure that the early Christians, from whom it all began and in whose honour this edifice and millions of others like it were erected, would have had no difficulty whatever in answering that question. To them it was abundantly simple. They followed a man of whom they'd known or heard at first hand, and who told them that His Kingdom was not of this world; and therefore the problem to them was an infinitely simple one. They didn't feel bound to relate their thoughts and their conduct to the permissive morality of the Court of the Emperor Nero. That was something that had nothing whatever to do with them. They didn't feel bound to associate themselves or attach themselves to political causes; they belonged to another world. Their cause was their love and loyalty to this Man. Even Peter on that tragic occasion when the cock crew knew exactly what he had done – denied an allegiance, an allegiance which was terrifically simple and meaningful.

Now of course today the situation is different. Two thousand years have passed. Churches have come and gone, theologies have been discussed and drafted and abandoned and re-discussed. In this Church today a creed will have been recited; a creed to which I myself could assent to barely one single proposition in honesty, and I still think and feel sufficiently a Protestant to believe that the worst thing that any man can do is to say he believes something which in fact he doesn't. You will gather from this how utterly unfitted I would have been to be ordained in the Anglican or any other church. Yet there remains – and this, to me, is the extraordinary part about it – a sheer enchantment in the Christian religion; in the personality around which it is built, and in the Gospels and the Apostles from which it has been derived – an enchantment which has miraculously (one can only use that word) survived through the centuries. What other document is there extant which can still be read and have this unbelievable enchantment about it? There is, in this story, in this Man, some incredible living message which one still senses, and then one tries to relate that message to the edifice of institutional religion, whatever it may be, and somehow the two don't connect.

I spent three weeks recently in a Cistercian Abbey for the banal purpose of making a film about an enclosed order. But, of course, one did live there; one did get some idea, a feel of what this way of life amounted to. One of the occasions which sticks in my mind as illustrating what I mean about the extraordinary enchantment of the Christian faith, was talking to a lay brother; one of those men that you rarely meet in younger generations who combined an utterly simple and certain faith with an enormously practical and sagacious and amusing disposition. He was in charge of the farming; the monks farmed about a thousand acres. It was the lambing season, and he was very, very keen on these lambs. He was sitting, talking and looking lovingly at them, and suddenly I grasped the phrase 'Agnus Dei' which I had heard in the chapel in the morning – 'the Lamb of God'. And I thought: surely this was perhaps the most extraordinary moment of all in human history, when men for the first time saw their God in the likeness of a lamb, instead of, as heretofore, in the image of power or wealth or sensuality or beauty; God was presented to them in the form of a lamb. And I told this to Brother Oliver, and somehow, in a way that I can't fully explain to you, I understood what was meant by the Incarnation; somehow this basic doctrine took on life as Brother Oliver and I contemplated together the sheer stupendousness historically of this moment.

Now I could go through the story and illustrate again and again this enchantment; this drama which pulls one up. I could relate it to the Crucifixion; itself another fantastic moment, when the sick joke of some Roman soldiers that led them to write a ribald legend above a dying man's head, 'King of the Jews', and to dress him up in a purple robe and put a crown of thorns on his head – that sick joke abolished for ever the validity of earthly authority. It was a most stupendous thing to happen and it lives on in the Cross, in this symbol of the Christian religion which has been spread to every corner of our world.

Similarly with the miracles. I was thinking about the miracle of the feeding of the five thousand, and suddenly I realised this: there was this Man preaching, this extraordinary Man, and there these people had collected to listen, and some of them had brought refreshments – you know how people do – and felt rather superior because they had something to eat, and thought how they'd bring their packages out and munch them. And then the words that this extraordinary Man was saying made it totally impossible for them to do that. They couldn't eat the food they had brought with that man speaking, and so they passed it round to be shared with all the others. Of course that might not be true, but if it were, it would be so much the more miraculous, because in point of fact a man whose words overcame the terrible imprisonment in our egos and greed which make life for us personally, and for the human race, such hell, would be performing an almost inconceivable miracle!

Then I was enormously interested in the temptations in the wilderness. The first of them was the temptation to turn stones into bread. Now that would be a terrific temptation to Oxfam and all the different charitable organisations, and to all the different political parties and institutions dedicated to improving human conditions. What a monstrous thing to refuse to turn stones into bread, if it were true that what's the matter with us is that we haven't got enough bread. But if what's the matter with us is that we don't understand, then how infinitely wise to resist the temptation! Again, the miracle of jumping off a building and not being hurt is almost like space travel; the same sort of thing as the so-called wonders of science. Why not do that and dazzle mankind, so that they fall down and worship? But that too was a temptation to be resisted, because, after all, the wonders of science are not so very wonderful, and only deserve worship if the infinitely more wonderful wonders of God – which include and transcend them – are overlooked. Finally, the most important of all, the temptation to take over the kingdoms of the earth. This is what all good progressive people are always trying to do – to take over the governments and make them good. What a monstrous thing from the point of view of, say, Canon Collins, to refuse to accept the government of the world! But, you see, at the same time, what an alluring and enchanting thing to do, because how awful it would be if it were really possible to make human life acceptable by simply making governments good! And how absolutely essential it was to demonstrate that merely having righteous government doesn't in itself, constitute living righteously.

I've said enough to show what I mean, I hope, about the incredible and inexhaustible enchantment of this religion.

Now there is the question I have to go on to if I am to ask myself, Am I a Christian? How is it that something so enchanting, something that seems to fit so perfectly into the situation in which human beings find themselves, should have become, on the one hand, a collection of remote and, to me, incomprehensible and unbelievable theological propositions, and, on the other, a sort of package of progressive and humane and enlightened sentiments which I call sometimes, when I find myself on the BBC's Meeting Point programme, 'soper opera'. As far as the theological propositions are concerned, it's not really for me to speak. I don't understand them, I don't see their importance, they mean absolutely nothing to me. It may be, of course, that, for instance, a concept like the Trinity is tremendously important, but anyway not to me, and I have just to put that aside. But the question of the Kingdom of Heaven on earth and the Kingdom of Heaven in Heaven does seem to me an absolutely crucial one. The appeal of Christianity, as I understand it, is that it offers man something beyond this world. It says to him that he must die in order to live, an extraordinary proposition to put before him. It tells him that he can never create peace or happiness for himself merely by perfecting his circumstances on this earth. It presents him, in other words, as a creature who intrinsically requires salvation. Now it would seem to me that the churches and those who present the Christian religion to us have moved entirely away from this attitude, and increasingly tell us that it is possible to make terms with this world.

Take one of my favourite characters, Bunyan's hero in *The Pilgrim's Progress* which is a superb image of human life. He is hurrying on through his mortal life. If you'd said to Bunyan, "But surely your Pilgrim ought to stop in Vanity Fair and ensure that it's turned into a co-operative enterprise, or that 'one man one vote' is introduced there before he hurries on," Bunyan would surely have thought that you'd taken leave of your senses. The essence of his

Pilgrim is that he is pushing on. I would suggest to you that Western Man has for the last hundred and fifty years lived through a period of utopianism, collective utopianism; that, from the time of Darwin particularly, he has believed that it's possible to construct for himself a Kingdom of Heaven on earth. When I was young, we believed that that Kingdom of Heaven on earth had been constructed in the USSR. There are those good earnest people who believed that that Kingdom of Heaven on earth could be constructed by means of a Welfare State through the Labour Party. (I would hope and believe that the present Prime Minister has effectively put paid to those hopes!) The people who crossed the Atlantic to America went with the idea that they were going to find a Kingdom of Heaven on earth in America.

Now what has happened, it seems to me, is that these utopian hopes – and it was perfectly human that they should have been entertained – have been completely demolished, and we are confronted with a sort of emptiness. The very material success of our world adds to that effect. We have everything that we want materially, and it ought to make us happy, but for some reason it doesn't. It should be the case that the places where all these material things are most available, and where the pursuit of happiness (that absurd and ironical phrase) is most ardently undertaken, should also be the places where human beings are most happy and most purposive and most zealous in their lives; and in fact it's not so. Something has gone wrong. It hasn't worked. The idea that human beings can achieve fulfillment on earth by satisfying their fleshly appetites and their egotistic impulses has simply not worked, and where it's most possible to satisfy them is precisely where it's worked least. This situation is of course enormously intensified by virtue of the fact that, at the same time, we have created like a Frankenstein monster an enormous apparatus of persuasion such as has never before been known on earth.

Now I've spent the last forty years working in this apparatus, and I know exactly how it works. I know the people who operate it and the aims it pursues; and what is the effect? The effect of it is simply this, that it says to those whom it influences – and its power is fantastic – it says to them in effect, 'Satisfy your greed, satisfy your sensuality, that is the purpose of life.' You have a situation which is so fantastic that it would be difficult to believe in it if one didn't know it existed, and which posterity will certainly find difficulty in believing in, if there is any posterity. You have in a small area of the world an economic system which only works in so far as it constantly increases its gross national product. This is our golden calf, and year by year it must get bigger. In order that its getting bigger shouldn't create chaos, people must constantly consume more and want more, so that we must dedicate some of our most brilliant talents and a huge proportion of our wealth to making them want what they don't want. It's the most extraordinary state of affairs. At the same time, while this is going on in one part of the world, in another part of the world people are getting poorer and poorer and hungrier and hungrier.

When I was in Detroit, Mr Reuther said to me that every year they must sell nine million new automobiles in the United States or the place goes bust. Imagine it, you must persuade nine million people to want a new automobile in order to survive. This is a completely crazy situation, and the sense of its craziness is precisely what is creating in human beings so tremendous a spiritual hunger. They know that it's not true that if you satisfy all people's material and physical wants you will make them serene and happy. They know that it's not working out, and so this produces in them a sense of total lostness and bewilderment. It seems to me absolutely clear that either they must recover a sense of what those early Christians had when they too found themselves in a world which was running into destruction and ruin, or the process goes on and produces catastrophe.

It's a perfectly simple choice, and the problem before us is how to present this Christian answer in such a way that people see how apposite it is. I don't know how that can be done. I see a world which is sailing under completely false colours, whose fantastic technological achievements have produced for it both plenty such as has never been known before and means of destruction such as has never been known before and boredom such as has never been known before. The only conceivable alternative to this materialist view of life is in some form or another the Christian view, but, as I have tried to indicate, this Christian view itself in the course of its presentation has got hopelessly caught up with the other.

Now what can one do? What can an individual do, faced with such a situation? I have one hero, a man called Paulinus who was born in the fourth century, and who came to realise that his civilisation was crashing to destruction. He decided that the only thing he could do was to keep alight a lamp in a particular shrine, and that's what he decided to do. It seems to me that that's all one can do, and that, in answer to this fantastic materialist view of life with this fantastic machine of persuasion behind it, the lamp should say to people that the opposite is true, that as the Christian religion taught originally, so it remains true that men can't live by bread alone, that men have to die in the flesh to be reborn in the Spirit, that men are not creatures of production whose existence can be measured by what they can produce or by what they can learn, but a family with a father in Heaven, and that the relationship between men is the relationship of brothers, and that each of them, in that he is loved by the father, must be in all senses the equal of every other, however he might differ in capacity or intelligence or beauty or anything else. All these things the lamp would say.

It might be just a forlorn enterprise; it might be that a materialist view of life will work out; that with the birth pill and nuclear weapons and the possibility of the gross national product endlessly increasing and of people endlessly able to satisfy all their desires, a sort of happiness could be produced. If it were so, it would seem to me the most pessimistic and terrible conclusion that could possibly be reached. And if it's not so, then my lamp, like Paulinus', would continue to shine when a darkness had fallen and a darkness which would be even deeper if it were to be associated, as it might be, with increasing technological development and efficiency. Such is the conclusion to which I've come, and whether it involves being a Christian or not I still don't know. It seems to me absolutely clear that there is only one answer to the deepening dilemma of contemporary materialism and that is essentially the answer set forth in the Christian religion namely, that men can never become natives of this earth, and that if they ever succeeded in so doing, then only would the light of divinity be finally put out in them.

A Sermon delivered at The University of Edinburgh Service in The High Kirk of St Giles', 14th January 1968.

THE ACTS OF THE APOSTLES

Chapter 17

Paul and Silas visit Thessalonica and are received by Jason:

Now when they had passed through Amphipolis and
Apollonia, they came to Thessalonica, where was a
synagogue of the Jews:
2. And Paul, as his manner was, went in unto them,
and three sabbath days reasoned with them out of the
scriptures.
3. Opening and alleging, that Christ must needs
have suffered, and risen again from the dead; and that
this Jesus, whom I preach unto you, is Christ.
4. And some of them believed, and consorted with
Paul and Silas; and of the devout Greeks a great
multitude, and of the chief women not a few.
5. But the Jews which believed not, moved with
envy, took unto them certain lewd fellows of the baser
sort, and gathered a company, and set all the city on
an uproar, and assaulted the house of Jason, and
sought to bring them out to the people.
6. And when they found them not, they drew Jason
and certain brethren unto the rulers of the city, crying,
These that have turned the world upside down are
come hither also;
7. Whom Jason hath received: and these all do
contrary to the decrees of Caesar, saying that there is
another king, one Jesus.

Another King

Nowadays when I occasionally find myself in a pulpit – one of those bad habits one gets into in late middle age – and never, by the way, in a more famous pulpit than this one, St Giles, Edinburgh, I always have the same feeling as I look round as I do now at your faces; a deep passionate longing to be able to say something memorable, to shed some light.

"I am the light of the world," the Founder of the Christian Religion said. What a stupendous phrase! And how particularly marvellous today when one is conscious of so much darkness in the world! "Let your light shine before men," he exhorted us.

You know, sometimes on foolish television or radio panels, or being interviewed, someone asks me what I most want, what I should most like to do in the little that remains of my life, and I always nowadays truthfully answer, and it is truthful, "I should like my light to shine even if only very fitfully, like a match struck in a dark cavernous night and then flickering out."

How I should love to be able to speak to you with even a thousandth part of the certainty and the luminosity of St Paul, when, as you heard in the lesson, he was speaking in Thessalonica. Golden words, a bright and shining light indeed. Now something had happened to him, as it had to Christ's disciples, transforming them from rather inarticulate, cowardly men who ran away for cover when their leader was arrested, into the most lion-hearted, eloquent, quick-witted, yes, and even gay evangelists the world has ever known. Irresistible in their oratory, indomitable in their defiance, captivating in their charm; overwhelming in the love which shone in their faces, in their words and in their deeds, so that, as we heard, in the most literal sense they turned the world upside down with their crazy allegiance to this other king, one Jesus. Well, what had happened to them? We can call it what we like as far as I'm concerned – 'the Holy Ghost descending,' 'Damascus Road conversion,' 'speaking with tongues,' anything you like, I don't mind. The point is that, as they said themselves, they were reborn. They were new men with a new allegiance, not to any form of earthly authority but to this other king, this Jesus. Ever since their time, with all the ups and downs, confusions and villanies of institutional Christianity, this notion has persisted, of being reborn, of dying in order to live, and I want to consider whether such a notion, as I understand it the very heart of the Christian religion, has any point or validity today.

In the boredom and despair of an expiring Roman civilisation with all the inevitable accompaniments of permissive morality, addiction to vacuous violence, erotic and narcotic fantasies, it offered a new light of hope, a new joy in living to one and all, including, perhaps especially including, the slaves. In our uncannily similar circumstances, has it anything to offer today? That's my question. Of course I can't answer it as St Paul and the disciples did. They were the beginning; we are the end.

I, too, belong to the twentieth century, with a twentieth century sceptical mind and sensual disposition, with the strange mixture of crazy credulity in certain directions, as for instance in science and advertising and equally crazy scepticism, so that illiterate schoolboys and half-baked university students turn aside with contemptuous disbelief before propositions which the greatest minds and the noblest dispositions of our civilisation accepted as self-evident. That is our twentieth century plight. Let me then, in true twentieth century style, begin with a negative proposition – what I consider to be the ineluctable unviability and absurdity of our present way of life.

How can anyone, apart from an occasional with-it cleric, Provost of King's or Hungarian economist, seriously believe that by projecting present trends into the future we arrive at enduring human felicity – producing more and more and consuming more and more year by year under the impetus of an ever more frenzied persuasion of mass communication media, and at the same time watching the rest of mankind get hungrier and hungrier, in even greater want; growing even stronger, with the means at our disposal to blow ourselves and our earth itself to smithereens many times over, and at the same time becoming ever more neurotic about the imminence of global nuclear war; moving ever faster and further afield, exploding the universe itself, and pursuing happiness, American style; "grinding out our appetites," as Shakespeare so elegantly put it, ever more desperately, with physical and even moral impunity, and spiritual desolation. It is a state of affairs at once so bizarre and so tragic that I alternate between laughing hilariously at it and looking forward eagerly to my departure, quite soon now – in at most a decade or so.

May I, moving from general things to more particular ones, consider for instance the situation in this ancient University, with which through the accident of election I find myself briefly associated. The students here in this university, as in other universities, are the ultimate beneficiaries under our welfare system. They are supposed to be the spearhead of progress, flattered and paid for by their admiring seniors, an elite who will happily and audaciously carry the torch of progress into the glorious future opening before them. Now speaking for myself, there is practically nothing that they could do in a mood of rebelliousness or refusal to accept the ways and values of our rundown, spiritually impoverished way of life for which I shouldn't feel some degree of sympathy or, at any rate, understanding, up to and including blowing up this magnificent edifice in which we are now assembled. Yet how infinitely sad; how, in a macabre sort of way, funny that the form their insubordination takes should be a demand for Pot and Pills, for the most tenth rate sort of escapism and self indulgence ever known! It is one of those situations a social historian with a sense of humour will find very much to his taste. All is prepared for a marvellous release of youthful creativity; we await the great works of art, the high spirited venturing into new fields of perception and understanding – and what do we get? The resort of any old, slobbering debauchee anywhere in the world at any time – Dope and Bed.

The feeling aroused in me by this, I have to confess, is not so much disapproval as contempt, and this, as you may imagine, makes it difficult, in fact impossible, for me as Rector to fulfil my functions. Here, if I may, I should like to insert a brief word of personal explanation. I, as Rector, and Allan Frazer as my Assessor, find ourselves as you know responsible for passing on to the university authorities the views and requests of the student body as conveyed to us by their elected officers, and as set forth in their magazine *Student* for whose conduct they are responsible. Their request concerning the birth pill is as it happens highly distasteful to us, as we have not hesitated to let it be known. The view of the SRC officers as expressed by some of them, and not repudiated publicly by any of them, is that the Rector and his Assessor are bound not only to pass on but to recommend whatever the SRC may decide. This is a role which, in my opinion, no self-respecting Rector, or Assessor, could possibly countenance, and I have therefore asked the Principal to accept my resignation, as has my Assessor. The ensuing Rectorial contest, when it takes place, will serve to show, as I hope, what calibre of candidate will come forward to contest the Rectorship on the terms laid down by the present SRC officers, and whether the views now put forward by them in fact enjoy the support of a majority of the students of Edinburgh University.

So, dear Edinburgh students, this may well be the last time I address you, and this is what I want to say – and I don't really care whether it means anything to you or not, whether you think there is anything in it or not. I want you to believe that this row I have had with your elected officers has nothing to do with any puritanical attitudes on my part. I have no belief in abstinence for abstinence's own sake, no wish under any circumstances to check any fulfilment of your life and being. But I have to say to you this: that whatever life is or is not about, it is not to be expressed in terms of drug stupefaction and casual sexual relations. However else we may venture into the unknown it is not I assure you on the plastic wings of *Playboy* magazine or psychedelic fancies.

I have recently, as you might have heard, been concerned in making some films for BBC Television on the New Testament, and it involved, along with much else, standing on what purports to be and, unlike most shrines, may well be the Hill of Beatitudes where the most momentous of all sermons was preached some two thousand years ago. It was rather marvellous standing there looking down on the Sea of Galilee and trying to reconstruct the scene – the obscure teacher and the small, nondescript, mostly illiterate crowd gathered round him. For the Christian religion began, let us never forget, not among brilliant, academic minds, not among the wealthy, or the powerful, or the brilliant, or the exciting, or the beautiful, or the fascinating, not among television personalities or leader-writers on *The Guardian;* it began among these very simple illiterate people, and one was tremendously conscious of them gathered there.

And then those words, those incomparable words, which were to echo and re-echo through the world for centuries to come, even now not quite lost. How it is the meek not the arrogant who inherit the earth. How we should love our enemies and do good to them that hate us. How it is the poor not the rich who are blessed, and so on. Words which have gone on haunting us all even though we ignore them; the most sublime words ever spoken.

One of the Beatitudes that had for some reason never before impressed me particularly this time stuck in my mind and has stayed there ever since. It is: "Blessed are the pure in heart for they shall see God." May I commend this Beatitude to you as having some bearing on our present controversies and discontents. To see God is the highest aspiration of man, and has preoccupied the rarest human spirits at all times. Seeing God means understanding, seeing into the mystery of things. It is, or should be, the essential quest of universities like this one, and of their students and their staff. Note that the realisation of this quest is achieved, not through great and good deeds, nor even through thought, however perceptive and enlightened, certainly not through sensations however generated, or what is called success however glittering. The words are clear enough – "Blessed are the pure in heart for they shall see God."

To add to the macabre comedy of our situation, into the ribald scene of confusion and human inadequacy that I have been talking about there break idiot voices prophesying a New Jerusalem just round the corner. One always, I find, underestimates the staying power of human folly. When poor old H.G. Wells breathed his last having produced, in *Mind at the End of its Tether,* a final hysterical repudiation of everything he had ever said or thought, I fondly supposed and said to myself that no more would be heard in my time of men like gods. How wrong I was. A quarter of a century later a Provost of King's, Cambridge was to carry the same notion to an even higher pitch of fantasy. No doubt, long after I am gone someone will be saying on some indestructible programme like "Any Questions" that a touch more abortion, another year at school and birth pills given away with the free morning milk and all will be well.

What are we to do about it, this crazy gadarene slide? I never met a man made happy by money or worldly success or sensual indulgence still less by the stupefaction of drugs or alcohol. Yet we all, in one way or another pursue these ends, as the advertiser well knows. He offers them in technicolour and stereosound, and there are many takers. The politician likewise often with a nondescript retinue of academic and clerical support, offers the same package in collective terms. Underneath, we all know how increasingly hollow and unconvincing it is – the great society, mankind coming of age, men like Gods, all the unspeakable cant of Utopians on the run. Our very art and literature, such as they are, convey the same thing, the bad dreams of a materialist society. Bacon and Pinter tapering off into the sheer incoherence of a Burroughs and a Beckett, with the Beatles dancing on our grave, and Alan Ginsburg playing his hand harmonium, and that delectable old Hindu con-man, the Maharishi, throwing in his blessing. Communist utopianism produced Stalin; the pursuit of happiness American style, produced Lyndon Johnson, and our special welfare variety has produced Harold. If that doesn't put paid to all three nothing ever will.

So I come back to where I began, to that other king, one Jesus; to the Christian notion that man's efforts to make himself personally and collectively happy in earthly terms are doomed to failure. He must indeed, as Christ said, be born again, be a new man, or he's nothing. So at least I have concluded, having failed to find in past experience, present dilemmas and future expectation any alternative proposition. As far as I am concerned, it is Christ or nothing.

To add a final touch of comic relief (because you know an ex-editor of *Punch* cannot help, even in the most gruesome situations, looking around for something comic) I might add that what I have just said, is, I know, far more repellent to most of the present ecclesiastical establishment than any profession of scepticism or disbelief. They find such an attitude pessimistic, though I wonder whether, in the history of all the civilisations that have ever been, a more insanely optimistic notion has ever been entertained than that you and I, mortal, puny creatures, may yet aspire with God's grace and Christ's help to be reborn into what St Paul calls "the glorious liberty of the children of God."

I increasingly see us in our human condition as manacled and in a dark cell. The chains are our mortal hopes and desires, the dark cell our ego, in whose obscurity and tiny dimensions we are confined. Christ tells us how to escape, striking off the chains of desire and putting a window in the dark cell through which we may joyously survey the wide vistas of eternity and the bright radiance of God's universal love. No view of life, as I am well aware, could be more diametrically opposed to the prevailing one today, especially as purveyed in our mass communication media, dedicated as they are to the counter proposition, that we can live by bread alone, and the more the better. Yet I am more convinced than I am in my own existence that the view of life Christ came into the world to preach, and died to sanctify, remains as true and as valid as ever, and that all who care to, young and old, healthy and infirm, wise and foolish, with or without 'A' or 'O' levels may live thereby, finding in our troubled, confused world, as in all other circumstances and at all other times, an enlightenment and a serenity not otherwise attainable. Even though, as may very well prove the case, our civilisation like others before it soon finally flickers out, and institutional Christianity with it, the light Christ shed shines as brightly as ever for those who seek an escape from darkness. The truths he spoke will answer their dilemmas and assuage their fears, bringing hope to the hopeless, zest to the despairing and love to the loveless, precisely as happened two thousand years ago and through all the intervening centuries.

I finished off my filming in the Holy Land by taking with a friend the road to Emmaus. Those of you who still read the Bible will remember the details – how shortly after the Crucifixion, Cleopas, some sort of relative of Christ's family, and a friend were walking from Jerusalem and inevitably talking as they went along about the Crucifixion which had happened so recently. They were joined by a third man who fell into step beside them and shared in their conversation. When they arrived at their destination in Emmaus, since it was late they pressed him to come and eat supper with them. The story, you know, is so incredibly vivid that I swear to you that no one who has ever tried to write can doubt its authenticity. There is something in the very language and manner of it which breathes truth. Any way, they went in to eat their supper, and of course when the stranger broke bread they realised he was no stranger but their Saviour. As my friend and I walked along like Cleopas and his friend, we recalled as they did the events of the Crucifixion and its aftermath in the light of our utterly different and yet similar world. Nor was it a fancy that we too were joined by a third presence ready to emerge from the shadows and fall in step along the dusty, stony way.

Malcolm Muggeridge clearly sees himself as a man in via. *Frankly he faces the mystery of death. But he is a man imbued with hope, "helped .... above all, by Jesus Christ .... helped, above all, by the Incarnation and all its consequences .... ."*

He is at one with a monk of the Orthodox Church who wrote: "For most Christians heaven is envisaged as a kind of postscript, an appendix to a book of which life on earth constitutes the actual text. But the contrary is true. Our earthly life is merely the preface to the book. Life in heaven will be the text – a text without end."

Donald Coggan

The Prospect of Death

The one sure thing about our mortal existence is that it will end; the moment we are born, we begin to die. The basic fact of death is today highly unpalatable, to the point that extraordinary efforts are made, linguistically and in every other way, to keep death out of sight and mind.

Mother Teresa, with characteristic audacity, calls the place where derelicts from the streets of Calcutta are brought by her Missionaries of Charity (actually a former Hindu temple), a home for dying destitutes, whereas the sanctuaries for the more affluent derelicts of the west are called rest homes. Even in the chillier world of hospitalisation, terminal ward is preferred to death ward, termination being scientific and so anodyne, unlike death which is fearsome and mysterious.

Even those who for one reason or another advocate killing off unborn children and the debilitated old seek to clothe their murderous intentions in elusive terms such as: "retrospective fertility control" for abortion, and "mercy killing" for euthanasia. A month spent in Florida in the company of fellow-geriatrics gave me some idea of the lengths to which the old are induced to go in order to distract their thoughts from their impending demise. In, let us call it, Sunshine Haven, everything was done to make us feel that we were not really aged, but still full of youthful zest and expectations; if not teen-agers, then keen-agers, perfectly capable of disporting ourselves on the dance-floor, the beach, or even in bed. Withered bodies arrayed in dazzling summer-wear, hollow eyes glaring out of garish caps, skulls plastered with cosmetics, lean shanks tanned a rich brown, bony buttocks encased in scarlet trousers – it all served to make a Florida beach on a distant view a macabre version of Keat's Grecian Urn:

> What men or gods are these? What maidens loath?
> What mad pursuit? What struggle to escape?
> What pipes and timbrels? What wild ecstasy?

Nearer at hand, the impression was more in the vein of Evelyn Waugh's *The Loved One.* At Forest Lawn, the original of Waugh's Whispering Glades, the cadavers are scented and anointed and dressed for their obsequies in their exotic best, down to underclothes; in Sunset Haven, pre-cadavers likewise array themselves for social occasions like young debutantes and their squires out on a spree, and behave accordingly, though sometimes with creaking joints and inward groans. Of all the amenities available in Sunset Haven – bingo, swimming pools, books, billiards and golf – the one never spoken of or advertised in any way is the crematorium, discreetly hidden away among trees and bushes, and unmentioned in the illustrated brochures. Yet evidently business is brisk through the winter months despite the sunshine and the geriatric *joi de vivre* so much in evidence. Death becomes the dirty little secret that sex once was; Eros comes out of hiding, and old Father Time tries to secrete his scythe.

Another method of, as it were, sweeping death under the carpet is to stow away the debilitated old in state institutions, where they live in a kind of limbo between life and death, heavily sedated and inert. Private institutions for the affluent old are naturally better equipped and staffed, but can be very desolating, too. Those under Christian auspices, especially when they are run by nuns, usually have long waiting lists, not so much because the prospective inmates are particularly pious, as because they want to be sure that some zealot for mercy-killing will not finish them off arbitrarily by administering excessive sedation; or, if they happen to need to be in an iron lung or attached to a kidney machine, by pulling the plug, as it is put in today's rather disgusting medical jargon.

In any case, disposing of people who live inconveniently long, and of defectives of one sort and another, has, from the point of view of governments, the great advantage of saving money and personnel without raising a public hullabaloo – something governments are always on the look out for. It is, of course, inevitable that, in a materialist society like ours, death should seem terrible, and even inadmissible. If Man is the very apex of creation, with nothing greater than himself in the universe; if his earthly life exhausts the whole content of his existence, then, clearly, his definitive end, his death, is too outrageous to be contemplated, and so is better ignored.

Simone de Beauvoir, in her book *A Very Easy Death,* describes her mother's death from cancer as being "as violent and unforeseen as an engine stopping in the middle of the sky." The image is significant; death is seen, not as the finale of a drama; nor as the end of an act, to be followed by a change of scene and the rest of the play; not even as an animal expiring, but as the breakdown of a machine which suddenly and maddeningly stops working. "There is no such thing as a natural death," Madame de Beauvoir concludes. "All men must die, but for every man his death is an accident, and, even if he knows it and consents to it, an unjustifiable violation." In the light of such an attitude, death becomes a monstrous injustice, an act of brutal oppression, like, say, the Vietnam War, or apartheid in South Africa. One imagines a demo led by Madame de Beauvoir, and all the demonstrators chanting in unison: "Death out! Death out!"

The slogan is not quite as preposterous as might at first glance be supposed; the crazy notion that some sort of drug might be developed which would make its takers immortal, a death-pill to match the birth-pill, has been seriously entertained. And how wonderfully ironical that *soma,* the drug in Aldous Huxley's *Brave New World* that was to make everyone happy for evermore, should have been the name originally chosen for thalidomide! Nor is it fanciful to detect in the mania for transplants of hearts, kidneys and other organs, perhaps even genitals, a hope that it may become possible to keep human beings going indefinitely, like vintage cars, by replacing their spare parts as they wear out.

Again, experimentation in the field of genetics would seem to hold out the prospect of being able in due course to produce forms of life not subject to death. Jonathan Swift, in *Gulliver's Travels,* showed a clearer sense of our true human condition when he made the immortal Struldbrugs, encountered by Gulliver on this third voyage to the flying island of Laputa, not, as Gulliver had supposed they would be, wise, serene and knowledgeable, but rather the most miserable of creatures, excruciatingly boring to themselves and to others. Whenever they see a funeral, Gulliver learns, they lament and repine that others are gone to a harbour of rest, to which they themselves never can hope to arrive.

Indeed, sanely regarded, death may be seen as an important factor in making life tolerable; I like very much the answer given by an octogenarian when asked how he accounted for his longevity – "Oh, just bad luck!" No doubt for this reason among others, death has often in the past been celebrated rather than abhorred; for instance, very exquisitely, by the Metaphysical Poets, among whom John Donne may be regarded as the very laureat of death. So alluring did he find the prospect of dying that when he was Dean of St Paul's he had himself painted in his shroud so as to be reminded of the deliverance from life that lay ahead. Sleep, he points out, even just for a night, wonderfully refreshes us; how much more, then, will sleeping on into eternity be refreshing! And then:

One short sleep past, we wake eternally,
And Death shall be no more, Death thou shalt die.

In our own time, Dietrich Bonhoeffer manifested a similar attitude to death when, with his face shining in joyful expectation, he said to the two Nazi guards who had come to take him to be executed: "For you it is an end, for me a beginning." Likewise Blake when, on his deathbed, he told his wife Catherine that to him dying was no more than moving from one room to another. As his end approached he sang some particularly beautiful songs, which, he told Catherine, were not of his composition, but came directly from Heaven.

Alas, I cannot claim total certainty of this order, and fall back on Pascal's famous wager, which requires us to bet on eternal survival or eternal extinction. Confronted with such a choice, as Pascal points out in his *Pensées,* the obvious course must be to back the former possibility, since then, "if you win, you win everything; if you lose, you lose nothing." So, I back eternal survival, knowing full well that if eternal extinction should be my lot, I shall never know that I have lost my bet, and taking no account of exotic notions like Reincarnation, or of the so-called 'evidence' provided by people who have been in a coma and imagined they were dead. The fact is that to know what being dead is like, you have to die, just as to know what being born is like you have to be born.

In support of my choice, I can say with truth that I have never, even in times of greatest preoccupation with carnal, worldly and egotistic pursuits, seriously doubted that our existence here is related in some mysterious way to a more comprehensive and lasting existence elsewhere; that somehow or other we belong to a larger scene than our earthly life provides, and to a wider reach of time than our earthly allotment of three score years and ten. Thus, death has seemed more alluring than terrible, even perhaps especially, as a belligerent of sorts in the 1939–45 war; for instance, wandering about in the London Blitz, and finding a kind of exaltation in the spectacle of a bonfire being made of old haunts like Fleet Street, Paternoster Row, the Inner Temple, as though, not only might I expect to die myself, but the world I knew, the way of life to which I belonged, was likewise fated to be extinguished. Now, death seems more alluring than ever, when, in the nature of things, it must come soon, and transmits intimations of its imminence by the aches and pains and breathlessness which accompany old age.

It has never been possible for me to persuade myself that the universe could have been created, and we, *homo sapiens,* so-called, have, generation after generation, somehow made our appearance to sojourn briefly on our tiny earth, the same characters and situations endlessly recurring, that we call history. It would be like building a great stadium for a display of tiddly-winks, or a vast opera house for a mouth organ recital.

There must, in other words, be another reason for our existence and that of the universe than just getting through the days of our life as best we may; some other destiny than merely using up such physical, intellectual and spiritual creativity as has been vouchsafed us. This, anyway, has been the strongly held conviction of the greatest artists, saints, philosophers and, until quite recent times, scientists, through the Christian centuries, who have all assumed that the New Testament promise of eternal life is valid, and that the great drama of the Incarnation which embodies it, is indeed the master-drama of our existence. To suppose that these distinguished believers were all credulous fools whose folly and credulity in holding such beliefs has now been finally exposed, would seem to me to be untenable; and anyway I'd rather be wrong with Dante and Shakespeare and Milton, with Augustine of Hippo and Francis of Assisi, with Dr Johnson, Blake and Dostoevsky than right with

Voltaire, Rousseau, the Huxleys, Herbert Spencer, H.G. Wells and Bernard Shaw.

It must be admitted that as the years pass – and how quickly they pass, their passing speeding up with the passage of time! – our world and living in it come to seem decidedly over-rated; as Saint Theresa of Avila put it, no more than a night in a second-class hotel. Even so, it is extraordinary how even in old age, when ambition is an absurdity, lechery a bad joke, cupidity an irrelevance – how even then I find myself, as the General Confession in the Book of Common Prayer puts it so beautifully, following too much the devices and desires of my own heart. Talking to the young I have noticed with wry amusement how they assume that round about the late sixties a kind of cut-off operates whereby the world, the flesh and the devil automatically lose their appeal. If only it were so!

The best I can hope for in my dotage is to emulate the state of mind of the Sage in Dr Johnson's *Rasselas*, reflecting that of his creator:

> My retrospect of life recalls to my view many opportunities of good neglected, much time squandered upon trifles and more lost in idleness and vacancy. I leave many great designs unattempted, and many great attempts unfinished. My mind is burdened with no heavy crime, and therefore I compose myself to tranquility; endeavour to abstract my thoughts from hopes and cares which, though reason knows them to be vain, still keep their old possession of the heart; expect with serene humility, that hour which nature cannot long delay; and hope to possess in a better stage, that happiness which here I could not find, and that virtue which here I have not attained.

Nonetheless, the mystery remains; and ever must. Some eight decades ago I came into the world, full of cries and wind and hiccups; now I prepare to leave it, also full of cries and wind and hiccups. Whence I came I cannot know, least of all in the light of contemporary myths like Darwinian evolution, Freudian psychology, situational ethics, Marxist prophesy, and so on – surely the most absurd ever. Whither I go, if anywhere, I can only surmise, helped thereto by the testimony of true visionaries like the author of the *Cloud of Unknowing*, Blake, Dostoevsky, and, of course, above, all Jesus Christ; by inspired works of art like Chartres Cathedral and the *Missa Solemnis*, by the dedicated lives of saints and mystics; above all, by the Incarnation and all its consequences, in history, in what we still call western civilisation, now toppling into its final collapse, in providing infallible signposts in the quest for God.

The hardest thing of all to explain is that death's nearness in some mysterious way makes what is being left behind – I mean our earth itself, its shapes and smells and colours and creatures, all that one has known and loved and lived with – the more entrancing; as the end of a bright June day somehow encapsulates all the beauty of the daylight hours now drawing to a close; or as the last notes of a Beethoven symphony manage to convey the splendour of the whole piece. Checking out of St Theresa's second-class hotel, as the revolving doors take one into the street outside, one casts a backward look at the old place, overcome with affection for it, almost to the point of tears.

So, like a prisoner awaiting his release, like a schoolboy when the end of term is near, like a migrant bird ready to fly south, like a patient in hospital anxiously scanning the doctor's face to see whether a discharge may be expected, I long to be gone. Extricating myself from the flesh I have too long inhabited, hearing the key turn in the lock of Time so that the great doors of Eternity swing open, disengaging my tired mind from its interminable conundrums, and my tired ego from its wearisome insistencies. Such is the prospect of death.

The Universe Provides a Stage: Jesus is the Play

The Holy Land is full of history, written in stones, and with the faces in the streets for alphabet. Yet it was not history I found there, but some other deeper and more exhilarating truth that lay beneath the stones, the faces and all the hubbub and the fraudulence.

I remember the precise moment of illumination very well. It was in the Church of the Nativity in Bethlehem. I was sitting in the crypt waiting for the time when the public were excluded and we could begin to film. Earlier in the day we had been filming in nearby fields where, reputedly, shepherds were tending their flocks when they heard the tidings of great joy, that a Saviour had been born in Bethlehem whom they would find there in a manger wrapped in swaddling clothes. Sure enough, in the fields there was a shepherd with his flock – sheep and goats duly separated, just as required. When he caught sight of us and our equipment he picked up one of his sheep in his arms, precisely as in the coloured pictures I remembered so well from Scripture lessons in my childhood. Then, when he had established his posture, and our cameraman was focusing for a shot, he put down the sheep and came forward to haggle over his fee.

It was after settling this unseemly transaction, and getting our footage of the shepherd and his flock, that we went into the Church of the Nativity, having the greatest difficulty in making our way because of the press of beggars and children offering picture postcards, rosaries and other souvenirs for sale.

Still smarting from their persistent importunity, I had found a seat in the crypt on a stone ledge in the shadow cast by the lighted candles which provided the only illumination. How ridiculous these so-called 'shrines' were! I was thinking to myself. How squalid the commercialism which exploited them! Who but a credulous fool could possibly suppose that the place marked in the crypt with a silver cross was veritably the precise spot where Jesus had been born? The Holy Land, as it seemed to me, had been turned into a sort of Jesusland, on the lines of Disneyland.

Everything in the crypt – the garish hangings which covered the stone walls, the tawdry crucifixes and pictures and hanging lamps – was conducive to such a mood. The essential point, after all, about Jesus's birth was its obscurity, which made a perfect contrast with an Aphrodite rising in all her beauty and splendour out of the sea, or an Apollo radiant and masterful even by comparison with his fellow deities. How foolish and inappropriate, then, even from the point of view of fabricating a shrine, to furbish up what purported to be Jesus's birthplace with stage effects, decking out his bare manger to look like a junk-shop crammed with discarded ecclesiastical bric-a-brac! Rather, the shrine should surely aim at accentuating the bareness, the lowliness, of the occasion it celebrated, so that the humblest, poorest visitor might know that the Son of God was born into the world in even humbler, poorer circumstances than his.

As these thoughts passed through my mind I began to notice the demeanour of the visitors coming into the crypt. Some crossed themselves; a few knelt down; most were obviously standard twentieth century pursuers of happiness for whom the Church of the Nativity was just an item in a sightseeing tour – as it might be the Taj Mahal, or the Chamber of Horrors in Madame Tussaud's Waxworks Show in London, or Lenin's embalmed corpse in his mausoleum in the Red Square in Moscow.

Nonetheless, as I observed, each face as it came into view was in some degree transfigured by the experience of being in what purported to be the actual scene of Jesus's birth. This, they all seemed to be saying, was where it happened; here He came into the world! here we shall find Him! The boredom, the idle curiosity, the vagrant thinking all disappeared. Once more in that place glory shone around, and angel voices proclaimed: "Unto you is born this day . . . . a Saviour, which is Christ the Lord!" thereby transforming it from a tourist attraction into an authentic shrine. "Where two or three are gathered together in my name," Jesus promised, "there I am in the midst of them." The promise has been kept even in the unlikeliest of places — His own ostensible birthplace in the crypt of the Church of the Nativity in Bethlehem.

Looking for Jesus in history is as futile as trying to invent a yardstick that will measure infinity, or a clock that will tick eternity. God moulds history to His purposes, revealing in it the Fearful Symmetry which is His language in conversing with men; but history is no more than the clay in which He works. Who would look for Michelangelo's *Pieta* in the quarry where the marble to make it was procured? Or for Shakespeare's King Lear in history? If this is true of mortal genius, how much more so when the artist is God Himself, concerned to send us a self-portrait in the lineaments, and using the language of mortality in order to open up for us new vistas of hope and understanding.

This was the Incarnation, described in the opening words of the Fourth Gospel, in a passage surely among the greatest ever to be written at any time or by any hand. From its triumphant opening: "In the beginning was the Word, and the Word was with God, and the Word was God," to its beautiful and comforting conclusion: "And the Word was made flesh, and dwelt among us . . . . full of grace and truth," it conveys with perfect clarity why the Incarnation had to be, and what it meant for mankind, at the time and forever after.

So the story of Jesus has to begin with the Incarnation; without it, there would be no story at all. Plenty of great teachers, mystics, martyrs and saints have made their appearance at different times in the world, and lived lives and spoken words full of grace and truth, for which we have every reason to be grateful. Of none of them, however, has the claim been made, and accepted, that they were Incarnate God. In the case of Jesus alone the belief has persisted that when He came into the world God deigned to take on the likeness of a man in order that thenceforth men might be encouraged to aspire after the likeness of God, reaching out from their mortality to His immortality, from their imperfection to His perfection.

It is written in the Old Testament that no man may see God and live; at the same time, as Kierkegaard points out, God cannot make man His equal without transforming him into something more than man. The only solution was for God to become man, which He did through the Incarnation in the person of Jesus. Thereby, He set a window in the tiny dark dungeon of the ego in which we all languish, letting in a light, providing a vista, and offering a way of release from the servitude of the flesh and the fury of the will into what St Paul called "the glorious liberty of the children of God."

This is what the Incarnation, realised in the birth of Jesus, and in the drama of His ministry, death and Resurrection was to signify. With it, Eternity steps into Time, and Time loses itself in Eternity. Hence Jesus; in the eyes of God, a man, and in the eyes of men, God. It is sublimely simple; a transcendental soap-opera going on century after century and touching innumerable hearts; from some bleak, lonely soul seeking a hand to hold when all others have been withdrawn, to vast concourses of joyful believers singing their *glorias,* their *kyries,* their *misereres.* There have been endless variations in the script, in the music, in the dialogue, but one thing remains constant – the central figure, Jesus.

After the great Jehovah before whose wrath even the Gentiles bow down, the Lamb of God; after the immutable Law handed down to Moses from on high, grace and truth embodied in a Gospel of love; after the Creation, the Incarnation, when the momentous announcement: *Fiat Lux!* which begins our human story finds its fulfillment in another: *Ecce Homo!* Let there be Light!, and then; Behold the Man! With the Light came the universe, and all its creatures, illimitable space to be explored, and the tiniest atoms to be broken down into yet tinier ones. With the Incarnation came the Man, and the addition of a new spiritual dimension to the cosmic scene. The universe provides a stage; Jesus is the play.

The exigencies of the play require that His birth shall be both miraculous and ordinary. Wise Men attend it, and also shepherds; a new star announces it, and yet it takes place in the lowliest of circumstances – in a manger, with the beasts of the field that are housed there looking on expressionlessly as Jesus emerges from his mother's womb. Gifts of gold, frankincense and myrrh signify a royal birth, the coming of a prince of the House of David; the homely greetings of the shepherds welcome a friend of the poor, the lowly and the oppressed – a man for others.

Similarly, Mary, in delivering Incarnate God into the dangerous world, has to be, at once, the most radiant and warm-blooded of mothers whose breasts gush with milk, and a virgin untouched by any sensual hand or carnal experience. The Holy Child has to come, fleshly, out of her flesh, and, at the same time, not through fleshly processes. As she proclaims in her *Magnificat,* God has regarded her lowliness, and made her blessed in the eyes of future generations, by bestowing upon her the inestimable privilege that in her womb the Incarnation happens.

Until comparatively recent times, Christians found little

difficulty in combining these two themes of perfect motherhood and perfect virginity. The Maddonas of the Middle Ages, endlessly painted, sculptured, celebrated in verse and prose and plainsong, are glowingly alive without being involved in our human concupiscence. One comes across them in obscure churches as in great cathedrals and abbeys – faces of transcendental beauty that are also enchantingly homely, and even droll, in wood and stone and marble; with candle flames flickering in front of them and flowers heaped before them, and figures kneeling, touched with wonder. Such faces, blending physical and spiritual beauty into a sort of celestial coquetry, are likewise to be seen among nuns – or were until they put aside their habits and rules to follow Demas and the fashions of this present world.

In humanistic times like ours, a contemporary virgin – assuming there are any such – would regard a message from the Angel Gabriel that she might expect to give birth to a son to be called the Son of the Highest as ill-tidings of great sorrow and a slur on the local family-planning centre. It is, in point of fact, extremely improbable, under existing conditions, that Jesus would have been permitted to be born at all. Mary's pregnancy, in poor circumstances, and with the father unknown, would have been an obvious case for an abortion; and her talk of having conceived as a result of the intervention of the Holy Ghost would have pointed to the need for psychiatric treatment, and made the case for terminating her pregnancy even stronger. Thus our generation, needing a Saviour more, perhaps, than any that has ever existed, would be too humane to allow one to be born; too enlightened to permit the Light of the World to shine in a darkness that grows ever more oppressive.

To a twentieth century mind the notion of a virgin birth is intrinsically and preposterously inconceivable. If a woman claims – such claims are made from time to time – to have become pregnant without sexual intercourse, no one believes her. Yet for centuries millions upon millions of people never doubted that Mary had begotten Jesus without the participation of a husband or lover. Nor was such a belief limited to the simple and unlettered; the most profound and most erudite minds, the greatest artists and craftsmen, found no difficulty in accepting the Virgin Birth as an incontestable fact – for instance, Pascal, who in the versatility of his gifts and the originality of his insights was regarded as the Aristotle of his time.

Are we, then, to suppose that our forebears who believed implicitly in the Virgin Birth were gullible fools, whereas we, who would no more believe in such notions than we would that the world is flat, have put aside childish things and become mature? Is our scepticism one more manifestation of our having – in Bonhoeffer's unfortunate phrase – come of age? It would be difficult to support such a proposition in the light of the almost inconceivable credulity of today's brainwashed public, who so readily believe absurdities in advertisements and in statistical and sociological prognostications before which an African witch-doctor would recoil in derision.

With Pascal it was the other way round; while accepting, with the same certainty as he did the coming of the seasons, the New Testament account of Jesus's birth, he had already seen through and scornfully rejected the pretensions of science. Now, three centuries later, his intuition has been amply fulfilled. The dogmatism of science has become a new orthodoxy, disseminated by the Media and a State educational system with a thoroughness and subtlety far exceeding anything of the kind achieved by the Inquisition; to the point that to believe today in a miraculous happening like the Virgin Birth is to appear a kind of imbecile, whereas to disbelieve in an unproven and unprovable scientific proposition like the Theory of Evolution, and still more to question some quasi-scientific shibboleth like the Population Explosion, is to stand condemned as an obscurantist, an enemy of progress and enlightenment.

Through the eye of faith, then, Jesus is seen as, at once, God and Man, as Mary is seen as, at once, Virgin and Mother. Suddenly, almost with a click, like a film coming into sync, everything has meaning, everything is real; and the meaning, the reality, shine out in every shape and sound and movement, in each and every manifestation of life, so that I want to cry out with the blind man to whom Jesus restored his sight: "One thing I know, that, whereas I was blind, now I see." How, I ask myself, could I have missed it before?

Wherever and in whatever circumstances Jesus was born, there was, we may be sure, a real baby, wrinkled and wizened and full of wind, as babies are, and a doting mother to offer her breast, and look down with pride and joy at the tiny head of the little creature ardently sucking at it. Though in our time motherhood has been greatly devalued, and the sick phrase 'unwanted child' been given currency, it still remains true, as any nurse or gynaecologist will confirm, that it is extremely rare for any child at the moment of birth to be other than wanted in its mother's eyes.

Once when I was in Calcutta with Mother Teresa she picked up one of the so-called 'unwanted' babies which had come into the care of her Missionaries of Charity. It had been salvaged from a dustbin, and was so minute that one wondered it could exist at all. When I remarked on this, a look of exultation came into Mother Teresa's face. "See," she said, "there's life in it!" So there was; and suddenly it was as though I were present at the Bethlehem birth, and the baby Mother Teresa was holding another Lamb of God sent into the world to lighten our darkness.

If God chose to become incarnate as Jesus, then His birth, whatever marvels may have accomplished it, must have had the same characteristics as any other; just as, on the Cross, the suffering of the man into whom the Bethlehem child grew must have been of the same nature as that of the two delinquents crucified beside Him. Otherwise,

Jesus's humanity would have been a fraud; in which case, His divinity would have been fraudulent, too. The perfection of Jesus's divinity was expressed in the perfection of His humanity, and vice versa. He was God because He was so sublimely a man, and Man because, in all His sayings and doings, in the grace of His person and words, in the love and compassion that shone out of Him, He walked so closely with God. As Man alone, Jesus could not have saved us; as God alone, He would not; Incarnate, He could and did.

It was fitting that I should have travelled to Lichfield on 22nd September 1984 to hear Malcolm Muggeridge deliver his presidential oration in the 200th anniversary year of Dr Johnson's death. For it was thanks to Malcolm that I first came to read Johnson, or rather to read about him in Boswell's life, subsequently becoming addicted to this best of all biographies and dependent on a regular 'fix'.

My conversion coincided with my first acquaintance with the books of Malcolm's old friend Hugh Kingsmill, who in turn had introduced Malcolm to Johnson, and this led eventually to my writing a book God's Apology *which is about the friendship between Malcolm, Kingsmill, and Hesketh Pearson and which naturally contains many references to Johnson.*

Once ingested, Johnson governs the thoughts of his disciples, especially those who like myself are suspicious of politicians. As Malcolm points out, his central message is that it is personal rather than public benevolence that counts in life. Another lesson is that the pursuit of truth, which is the aim of all good journalists, can only be engaged in when, as Johnson advised, the mind has been cleared of 'cant'. Like Johnson, Malcolm has known what it is to be melancholy; he has also glimpsed the abiding truth of Christianity. Like Johnson too, I should add, Malcolm is a very charitable man, who has helped many obscure and unhappy people with his kindness and generosity. I myself shall always be grateful to him for his friendship and guidance.

Richard Ingrams

Dr Johnson Looks Heavenward

Ladies and gentlemen, I am greatly honoured to be asked to deliver the Presidential Address on the occasion of Dr Johnson's bicentenary. It is not just the occasion but the inexhaustible fascination of Dr Johnson himself that makes such an assignment pleasurable as well as honourable. I have often wondered what it is in Dr Johnson that makes him seem to me, and to many, many others, one of the most estimable of Englishmen. Of course he has a special appeal to any journalist; the trade or writing against time for money is one that he has glorified, both by practising it with consummate skill, and by describing its ardours with understanding and compassion. What reviewer of books, confronted with an unappetising volume, can resist echoing Dr Johnson's remark about Congreve's novel *Incognito or Love and Duty Reconciled,* that he "would rather praise it than read it?" What scribbler, late with delivery of his copy, will not indulge in a quiet chuckle over Dr Johnson's retort to the bookseller who, having handed him a subscription for his long-awaited edition of Shakespeare, asked that his name might be included in the printed list of the other subscribers. "Sir," Dr Johnson replied, "I have two very cogent reasons for not printing any list of subscribers – one that I have lost all their names, the other that I have spent all the money."

But there is more to it than this, I am sure. He loved truth as few have loved it, and could not endure even the most seemingly harmless deviations. His charity was inexhaustible, and his furious verbal assaults were invariably directed against what struck him as being hypocritical or false. I think no one ever appealed to him for help in vain; I think, equally, that he never once indulged in the sanctimonies of benevolence. How he trounced Mrs Thrale when she quoted with approval Garrick's egregious line, "I'd smile with the simple and feed with the poor!":

> Nay, my dear Lady, this will never do. Poor David! – Smile with the simple; what folly is that? And who would feed with the poor that can help it? No, no; Let me smile with the wise, and feed with the rich.

Garrick, I may add, was seldom away from the tables of the rich, and Mrs Thrale kept one herself, but Johnson characteristically gathered round him a weird little company of the outcast and the poor to sit at his table.

There are two aspects of Dr Johnson's life that have, for me, a special appeal – his journalism, what St Augustine of Hippo calls so aptly being a 'vendor of words', and his undeviating devotion to Christ, Christianity and Christendom. As far as the journalism is concerned, the scenario is a standard one; for instance, Dr Johnson writing that enchanting story, *Rasselas,* to pay for his mother's funeral, with a boy standing by to take the copy to the printer sheet by sheet as they become available. I can recall many such experiences, particularly in the matter of obituaries; those set in authority over us have a way of dying without warning in unreachable places at unseasonable times, leaving the poor obituarist to recount between editions their many and great services to the State. Nowadays, I expect, such situations scarcely arise; the computer does it all.

Then there was the matter of the parliamentary debates as reported by Dr Johnson in the *Gentleman's Magazine,* and much appreciated by its readers. In fact, he made up the speeches by Noble Lords and Honourable Members, having no opportunity to listen to them in either of the two Houses of Parliament. This came out when at a dinner party one of Pitt's speeches was highly praised, and Dr Johnson, who was present, let out that he had written the speech in a garret in Exeter Street. He added that in his sham reporting he managed to keep up appearances fairly well, but nonetheless ensured "that the whig dogs should not have the best of it." What, however, appalled him was the discovery that his readers were actually *believing* his reports to be true. Dr Johnson felt so strongly about this that he at once stopped writing his parliamentary reports, to the considerable chagrin of Cave who published them and benefited from their popularity. It was of Cave that Dr Johnson said "he had no relish for mirth but he could bear it" – an observation calculated to stir up memories of a sometime Editor of *Punch.* Supposing a similar attitude to Dr Johnson's prevailed today, why Fleet Street would soon empty, the TV screens all black out and the radio transmitters go silent. What, I wonder, would Dr Johnson make of the fantasy world the media have brought about whereby the cry of the Horrid Sisters in *Macbeth,* 'Fair is foul and foul is fair', becomes an acceptable slogan? Something pretty horrendous, I should suppose.

The documentation of Dr Johnson's life is extremely full. There is his assiduous biographer, James Boswell, who travelled with him, listened to him, stirred up his indignation like a matador with his Bull. Also Mrs Thrale, who subsequently became, to Dr Johnson's great indignation, Mrs Piozzi. She knew him intimately, loved him dearly, and recorded her memories of him truthfully and affectionately. There were biographers and numerous reminiscent friends such as Sir John Hawkins, Anna Seward, Arthur Murphy, not to mention the Doctor's own memories, which were liable to pop up, for instance in his *Lives of the Poets* and accounts of his travels.

There is, however, one aspect of Dr Johnson's life, and

that a vital one, which is for the most part only superficially conveyed by his friends and biographers – his religion. They knew well enough how seriously he took his religion, if only because of the way he silenced anyone who ventured in his company to introduce an element of facetiousness into a religious discussion. At the time of his death in 1784, he was collecting together prayers he had written down with a view to publishing them, but he died before the task was satisfactorily completed. Even so, the collection of prayers was there, and was subsequently deposited in the library of Pembroke College, Oxford, where Dr Elton Trueblood had access to them sorting them out and arranging them with suitable headings so that they may be read and studied, not just as individual prayers, but as the story of Dr Johnson's inward or spiritual life as distinct from his outward and intellectual life. Blake writes of a Golden String which we must follow:

> I give you the end of a Golden String,
>   Only wind it into a ball,
> It will lead you in at Heaven's Gate
>   Built in Jerusalem's Wall.

The sequence of prayers that Dr Johnson wrote, and that Dr Trueblood has arranged, may be seen as a verbal Golden String, leading, like the others, to Heaven's Gate in Jerusalem's Wall.

I have the good fortune to know Dr Trueblood, a fine scholar and a devout Christian. His handling of the Prayers relates them to one another and to Dr Johnson's own circumstances and aspirations. They are collected into one small volume, with a helpful introduction by Dr Trueblood which sets the scene. Dr Johnson's religious concern began in 1729 when he was twenty, and continued till his death at seventy-five. The spirit of the age, rather like ours, encouraged scepticism, to the point of assuming that all intelligent people found Christian zeal just amusing. In those days too they had their Don Cupitts. Dr Johnson's piety somehow transcends all this. In his essays he has to take account of the sceptical spirit of the age; in his prayers he is concerned only with his relationship with his Creator and the well-being, spiritual and physical, of those who were dear to him. Thus he prays that he may be delivered from carnal thoughts and impulses, that he may be more regular and assiduous in his work, that however afflicted his body may be God will spare his understanding. Dr Trueblood quotes him as saying in the last paragraph of the last issue of *The Rambler,* a periodical he founded, "The essays professedly serious, if I have been able to execute my own intentions, will be found exactly conformable to the precepts of Christianity and without any accommodation to the licentiousness and levity of the present age."

In a materialist society prayers tend to be a kind of celestial shopping-list; they ask on high for favours, and glory in reminiscences of special responses, sometimes pecuniary, that may have been received. Dr Johnson's prayers are more in the vein of waiting on God; they offer penitence rather than asking for this or that, and earnestly seek help in extricating themselves from any worldly or carnal pursuits in which they may have been involved. In his poem *Prayer* George Herbert assembles a dazzling array of poetic images:

Prayer, the Church's banquet, Angels' age,
  God's breath in man returning to his birth,
  The soul in paraphrases, heart in pilgrimage,
The Christian plummet, sounding heaven and earth;
Engine against the Almighty, sinner's tower.
  Revered thunder, Christ-side-piercing spear,
  The six-days' world transposing in an hour.
A kind of tune, which all things hear and fear;
Softness, and peace, and joy, and love, and bliss,
  Exalted manna, gladness of the best,

Heaven in ordinary, man well drest,
The milky way, the bird of paradise.
Church-bells beyond the stars heard, the soul's blood,
The land of spices, something understood.

As for waiting on God:

How, then, with fantasy pouring in continuously and variously from every direction, is it possible to find, and to hold on to, reality? I have found, or perhaps I may say been shown, a way which, somewhat diffidently, I herewith describe. First, quite deliberately, make a little clearing in the dark jungle of our ego and will in order to let in light. This involves much cutting down of nettles and brambles, for which I recommend wearing gloves. Then, with patience and true humility, wait on God (note 'on' not 'for'), whose presence, when it comes, as it assuredly will, brings everything into sync. So that out of confused sounds, words with a meaning emerge, and confused happenings sort themselves out and become recognisable. In other words, what seemed to be a Theatre of the Absurd, as Shakespeare puts it, full of sound and fury, signifying nothing, becomes a Theatre of Fearful Symmetry, in which the stage is the universe, and the cast is all mankind, and all the action, be it as minute as a leaf falling, or as far-reaching as a journey to the moon, has its own being and significance as belonging to God's creation, and so being a participant in His purpose for it.

A criticism that is lodged against Dr Johnson is that he is given to melancholy. This, up to a point, is true; he has found life in some respects disappointing, and anyway the cult of cheerfulness is not one that appeals to him. Apart from any other consideration, it conflicts with Christianity, which, as he understands it, is based on a man being crucified, and has taken the Cross as its symbol, in this going right back to the Apostle Paul. His attitude towards the settlers across the Atlantic Ocean in what is now the United States is far from sympathetic. "How is it," he asks, thinking of the role of the slave-traders in the newly developing country, "that we hear the loudest yelps for liberty come from the drivers of slaves?" No answer to his question was forthcoming then, or ever has been. There still lingered about inside him a dream of being offered some distinguished post like an embassy or the governorship of a colonial territory. Boswell, sensing this, took upon himself to remark to Dr Johnson that he wondered how so distinguished a citizen, now provided with a State pension, should be overlooked when it came to filling important posts. All he got in reply was a growl – "You may wonder, Sir." Dr Johnson had provided himself with his own cover-up in the shape of the carefully phrased farewell words of the Sage in *Rasselas.* He had just been told by Imlac that he might at least recreate himself with the recollection of an honourable and useful life, and enjoy the praise which all agree is due to him:

> 'Praise', said the sage, with a sigh, 'is to an old man an empty sound. I have neither mother to be delighted with the reputation of her son, nor wife to partake the honours of her husband. I have outlived my friends and my rivals. Nothing is now of much importance; for I cannot extend my interest beyond myself. Youth is delighted with applause, because it is considered as the earnest of some future good, and because the prospect of life is far extended: but to me, who am now declining to decrepitude, there is little to be feared from the malevolence of men, and yet less to be hoped from their affection or esteem. Something they may yet take away, but they can give me nothing. Riches would now be useless, and high employment would be pain. My retrospect of life recalls to my view many opportunities of good neglected, much time squandered upon trifles, and more lost in idleness and vacancy. I leave many great designs unattempted, and many great attempts unfinished. My mind is burdened with no heavy crime,

> and therefore I compose myself to tranquillity; endeavour to abstract my thoughts from hopes and cares, which, though reason knows them to be vain, still try to keep their old possession of the heart; expect, with serene humility, that hour which nature cannot long delay; and hope to possess, in a better state, that happiness which here I could not find, and that virtue which here I have not attained.'

These are Dr Johnson's splendid words, and my soul echoes them. Nonetheless, it has to be admitted that he was terrified at the prospect of death, not because it meant the end of earthly living; rather because by his own estimation there was the possibility of finding himself in Hell. It was his sins rather than the termination of his mortal existence that troubled him; in particular three of the Seven Deadly Sins – lust, gluttony and sloth. The last of these has a special association with writers. Who among them has not experienced the agony of hours, and sometimes days, with pen and paper ready to hand, an assignment unfulfilled and no words coming?

Also there is the question of Dr Johnson's mental condition. Certain eccentricities of behaviour and speech gave the impression that he was deranged, and perhaps mad. Indeed, with his scrofula and bad eyesight when he was born, in present circumstances there would have been a strong case for doing away with him at birth. Dr Johnson's own tolerance of eccentricity is well exemplified by a conversation he had with Dr Burney about the poet Christopher Smart who was supposed to be mad. "I do not think he ought to be shut up," Dr Johnson said. "His infirmities are not noxious to society. He insists on people praying with him, and I'd as lief pray with Kit Smart as anyone else. Another charge is that he does not love clean linen, and I have no passion for it myself." In the case of Dr Johnson's alleged madness, the suggestion has been made that when he was staying at Streatham as guest of the

Thrales, he was subjected to some sort of beating treatment by Mrs Thrale. This strikes me as absurd.

One thing, ladies and gentlemen, seems to me to be certain; in Lichfield Dr Johnson will go on being remembered, not so much for his achievements as a writer as for the mysterious quality of greatness that he exudes. I like to think of him myself, not so much for what he has undoubtedly achieved, his *oeuvre,* some twenty volumes, his travels so well described, his conversation and observations recorded by Boswell and others, but rather in Bolt Court with the strange miscellany of people he assembled there. First, Robert Levet, described as a practiser in physic, on whose death Dr Johnson wrote some beautiful lines:

Well tried through many a varying year,
See Levet to the grave descend,
Officious, innocent, sincere,
Of every friendless name the friend ....

No summons mock'd by chill delay,
No petty gain disdain'd by pride;
The modest wants of every day
The toil of every day supplied.

His virtues walked their narrow round,
Nor made a pause, nor left a void;
And sure th' Eternal Master found
The single talent well employ'd.

Along with him was Mrs Williams, a blind lady, about whom Boswell complained that when dispensing tea she used her finger to find out when the cups were full – a fastidiousness which came ill from Boswell in the light of complaints he had acquired in the course of his debaucheries. Then there were Pol Carmichael, "a Scotch wench", and Mrs Desmoulins, Presumably of French descent. Finally, there was Frank, Dr Johnson's black servant, who served him faithfully over a number of years, and to whom the Doctor bequeathed whatever he possessed at the time of his death. There was no apartheid in Bolt Court.

By the deathbed of Catherine Chambers, a servant for many years in his mother's household, Dr Johnson is quite at his best. Alone with her, and kneeling by her, he prays that "the sense of her weakness may add strength to her faith, and seriousness to her repentence." Together, they hope to meet again in a better place; then kiss and part. As his old friends die off he mourns for them; in the case of Garrick producing a superb requiem: "But what are the hopes of men? I am disappointed by that stroke of death which has eclipsed the gaiety of natoons, and impoverished the public stock of harmless pleasure. His "Life of Savage" in his *Lives of the Poets,* one of his finest achievements, concludes with a masterly sentence: "Those are no proper judges of his (Savage's) conduct who have slumbered away their time on the down of plenty, nor will any wise man presume to say, 'Had I been in Savage's condition, I should have lived or written better than Savage.' "

In his last illness he will accept no drugs so that he may meet his Maker with a clear mind. Here is his last prayer, which, as an octogenarian, I take on as my own:

> Almighty and most merciful Father, I am now as to human eyes it seems, about to commemorate, for the last time, the death of thy son Jesus Christ our Saviour and Redeemer. Grant, O Lord, that my whole hope and confidence may be in his merits, and his mercy; enforce and accept my imperfect repentence; make this commemoration available to the confirmation of my faith, the establishment of my hope, and the enlargement of my charity, and make the death of thy Jesus Christ effectual to my redemption. Have mercy upon me, and pardon the multitude of my offences. Bless my friends; have mercy upon all men. Support me, by the grace of thy Holy Spirit, in the

days of weakness, and at the hour of death, and receive me, at my death, to everlasting happiness, for the sake of Jesus Christ. Amen.

The nature and purpose of sexual activity, the family, human dignity, the fatherhood of God, life itself, these are some of the matters touched upon by Malcolm Muggeridge in his essay on the Encyclical, Humanae Vitae. *Much to be commended is the way he insists on the prophetic truth of its teaching, which may not be totally recognised by this generation. Yet, beyond the negative and destructive phenomena of our times, Malcolm Muggeridge emphasises the beauty and goodness of God's purposes for His creation and mankind's participation in that process. There is hope for all because 'God so loved the world that He sent His only Son' (Jn.3.16).*

Rt.Rev. Cormac Murphy-O'Connor

On Humanae Vitae *was the keynote address to a symposium on the document at the University of San Francisco delivered in July 1978.*

On *Humanae Vitae*

I find myself in a way in a curious position. After all, I'm not a Catholic. I haven't that great satisfaction that presumably most of you have. At the same time, I have a great love for the Catholic Church, and I've had from the beginning a feeling stronger than I can convey to you that this document, *Humanae Vitae,* which has been so savagely criticised, sometimes by members of your church, is of tremendous and fundamental importance, and that it will stand in history as tremendously important. And that I would like to be able to express, and I'm happy to have occasion this evening to express, this profound admiration that I have for it; this profound sense that it touches upon an issue of the most fundamental importance and that it will be, in history, something that will be pointed to both for its dignity and for its perspicuity.

It happens, ten years ago, that I found myself in the position of introducing a discussion on *Humanae Vitae* in a BBC television programme on a Sunday evening. And I can remember it very vividly. The people who are assembled for these discussions or panels on the BBC fall, usually, into various categories which are invariable: you generally have a sociologist from Leeds; you also have a life-purist usually with a moustache; you also have a knock-about clergyman of no particular denomination and enormous muttonchop whiskers; and you have, I regret to say, also, usually, a rather dubious father, which we had on this occasion, when I really very much wanted to have someone who was a passionate supporter of *Humanae Vitae*. However, I did have someone whom you're going to be fortunate enough to hear in the course of this symposium, and that was Dr Colin Clark, who has so marvellously and effectively dealt with what I consider to be one of the great con tricks in this whole controversy of contraception and related matters: the population explosion. So he was a great solace and comfort.

And then, in the course of presenting the programme, something happened which gave me inconceivable delight and which was also, in its way, extremely funny (because I often think that the mercy and wisdom of God comes to us more in humorous episodes than in solemn ones). In this programme, as the various people spoke for the first time, a short description of them was appended. And there had been prepared, to append to Dr Colin Clark's appearance, "Father of eight." But by a happy chance, this description got shifted to the "dubious father," so that he appeared on the programme as a father of eight. You must agree with me that somewhere or other there is the hand of a loving God who also has, as an all-loving God must necessarily have to look after a human race such as ours, a tremendous sense of humour. Anyway, that was that.

Now, tonight I find myself, ten years later, in the position of being responsible for what is called the "keynote address." And after thinking about it and scribbling down a few notes (that I'm glad to say I haven't brought with me), I wondered what sort of a keynote address I could hope to present to a gathering, most of whose members would certainly know far more about the matter under discussion than I do, and be far better versed in assembling the pros and cons of it.

And then, a rather interesting and, indeed, uplifting thought struck me, that of course I couldn't hope to deliver a keynote address on this particular subject because the keynote address had already been delivered two thousand years ago.

In other words, this matter which, as I've said, is of such tremendous importance, is an integral part of the relevation that came into the world in the Holy Land, that stupendous drama which has played such a fantastic role in the story of two thousand years of Christendom: the birth, the ministry, the death, and the resurrection of Jesus Christ as recounted in the Gospels. That was the keynote address for the matter before us this evening.

And after all, that keynote address, having been given to the world in those marvellous words of the fourth Gospel that the Word that became flesh and dwelt among us, full of grace and truth; that Word, that keynote address for all the centuries of our Western civilisation was itself carried by the Apostle Paul to a Roman world which was as bored, as derelict, as spent, as our civilisation often seems today. Carried to it, to animate it, to bring back the creativity which had been lost, to fill the world with great expressions in music, in architecture, in literature, in every sort of way, of this great new revelation.

Now why do I think that this was veritably our keynote address? Because, in that revelation, an integral part of that revelation – also something that was wonderfully novel and fresh to a tired and jaded world – was the sacramental notion. So that out of, for instance, the simple need of men to eat and drink came the Blessed Sacrament; and similarly, out of the creativity in men, their animal creativity, came the sacrament of love; the sacrament of love which created the Christian notion of family, of the marriage which would last, which would be something stable and wonderful in our society, out of which it came, and which has endured through all those centuries until now when we find it under attack. In my opinion, what has brought about, in the first case, this great weakening of the marvellous sacrament of reproduction, has been precisely what *Humanae Vitae* attacks and disallows. The procedures whereby eroticism, by its condition which is lasting love, becomes relegated to be a mere excitement in itself. And thereby are undermined not just relations between this man and that woman, but the whole shape and beauty and profundity of our Christian life.

Humanae Vitae recognised this and asked of Catholics what many of them were unable to accord, that they should not fall into this error, that they should eschew this dangerous procedure which was now being made available in terms at once infinitely simple, but also infinitely more dangerous, namely, the birth pill. Now whether, and how far, and to what extent this inhibition is or can be or will be acceptable, it's not for me to say. What I want to say tonight, as a non-Catholic, as an aspiring Christian, as someone who, as an old journalist, has watched this process of deterioration in our whole way of life – what I want to say is that in that encyclical the finger is pointed on the point that really matters: namely, that through human procreation the great creativity of men and women comes into play, and that to interfere with this creativity, to seek to relate it merely to pleasure, is to go back into pre-Christian times and ultimately to destroy the civilisation that Christianity has brought about.

That is what I want to testify to, as just one individual who has been given the great honour of coming and starting off your discussions. If there is one thing I feel absolutely certain about, it is that. One thing that I know will appear in social histories in the future is that the dissolution of our way of life, our Christian way of life and all that it has meant to the world, relates directly to the matter raised in *Humanae Vitae.*

The journalists, the media, write and hold forth about the various elements in the crisis of the Western world today: about inflation, about over-population, about pending energy shortages, about detente, about hundreds of things. But they overlook what your Church has not overlooked, this basic cause: the distortion and abuse of what should be the essential creativity of men and women, enriching their lives, as it has and does enrich people's lives – and when they are as old as I am, enriches them particularly beautifully, when they see as they depart from this world their grandchildren beginning the process of living which they are ending. There is no beauty, there is no joy, there is no compensation that anything could offer in the way of leisure, of so-called freedom from domestic duties, which could possibly compensate for one-thousandth part of the joy that an old man feels when he sees this beautiful thing: life beginning again as his ends, in those children that have come into the world through his love and through a marriage which has lasted through fifty and more years. I assure you that what I say to you is true, and that when you are that age there is nothing that this world can offer in the way of success, in the way of adventure, in the way of honours, in the way of variety, in the way of so-called freedom, which could come within a hundredth part of measuring up to that wonderful sense of having been used as an instrument, not in the achievement of some stupid kind of personal erotic excitement, but in the realisation of this wonderful thing – human procreation.

Now, of course, when *Humanae Vitae* was published to the world, and was set upon by all the pundits of the media, it was attacked as being a failure to sympathise with the difficulties of young people getting married. That was the basis on which the attack was mounted. But, it was perfectly obvious, and Colin Clark will remember from that symposium, with which the coming of *Humanae Vitae* was celebrated by the BBC – it was mentioned then that contraception was something that would not just stop with limiting families. That in fact, it would lead inevitably, as night follows day, to abortion and then to euthanasia. And I remember that the panel jeered when I said particularly the last, euthanasia. But it was quite obvious that this would be so. That if you once accepted the idea that erotic satisfaction was itself a justification, then you had to accept also the idea that if erotic satisfaction led to pregnancy, then the person concerned was entitled to have the pregnancy stopped. And, of course, we had these abortion bills that proliferated through the whole Western world. In England, we have already destroyed more babies than lives were lost in the first World War. Through virtually the whole Western world there now exists abortion on demand. The result has been an enormous increase in the misery and unhappiness of individual human beings and again, the enormous weakening of this Christian family.

I should mention to you that the point has been reached in England where a bishop has actually produced a special prayer to be used on the occasion of an abortion. You know, one of the great difficulties in being editor of *Punch* was something that I hadn't envisaged when I took the job on. And that is that whenever you tried to be funny about somebody, you would invariably find that something they actually did was funnier than anything that you could possibly think of. I really don't know how you could get a better example of it than a bishop solemnly setting to work to produce a measured prayer on the occasion of murdering a baby. But that is actually what has happened.

Now we move on to the next stage in this dreadful story. And it's all this that is implicit in the encyclical we're talking about. If it is the case that the only consideration that arises is the physical well-being of individual people, then what conceivable justification is there for maintaining at great expense and difficulty the people who are mentally handicapped, the senile old. I myself have long ago moved into what I call the "NTBR belt." And the reason I call it that is because I read about how a journalist who had managed to make his way into a hospital ward had found that all the patients in the ward who were over sixty-five had "NTBR" on their medical cards. And when he pressed them to tell him what these initials stood for, he was told "Not to be resuscitated."

Well I've been in that belt for some ten years, so I know

that as sure as I can possibly persuade you to believe, this is what is going to happen: governments will find it impossible to resist the temptation with the increasing practice of euthanasia, though it is not yet officially legal, except in certain circumstances I believe, for instance, in this state of California. The temptation will be to deliver themselves from this burden of looking after the sick and imbecile people or senile people, by the simple expedient of killing them off. Now this, in fact, is what the Nazis did. And they did it, not as is commonly suggested, through slaughter camps and things like that, but by a perfectly coherent decree with perfectly clear conditions. And, in fact, it is true that the delay in creating public pressure for euthanasia has been due to the fact that it was one of the war crimes cited at Nuremburg. So, for the *Guinness Book of Records,* you can submit this: that it takes just about thirty years in our humane society to transform a war crime into an act of compassion. That is exactly what happened.

So you see, the thought, the prayer, the awareness of reality behind *Humanae Vitae* has, alas, been amply born out precisely by these things that have been happening. I feel that Western man has come to a sort of parting of the ways (and that as time goes on you who are much younger will realise this), in which these two ways of looking at our human society will be side by side, and it will be necessary to choose one or the other. On the one hand, the view of mankind which has all through the centuries of Christendom been accepted in one form or another by Western people: that we are a family; that mankind is a family with God who is the father. In a family you don't throw out the specimens that are not up to scratch. In a family you recognise that some will be intelligent and some will be stupid, some will be beautiful and some will be ugly. But what unites the family is the fatherhood of God.

Now, what our way of life is now moving towards is the replacement of this image of the family by the image of a factory farm in which what matters is the economic prosperity of the family and of the livestock, so that all other considerations cease to be relevant. And you will find that this terrible notion increasingly occupies the minds of people and becomes acceptable to them.

There is something else that is envisaged in the encyclical that we are talking about. I wanted to say to you how desperately sorry I am that Mother Teresa won't be here at this gathering. Partly because it's always an infinite joy for me to see her, because it would have been an infinite joy for you to hear her, but also because her feelings about what I'm talking are of the strongest and the deepest, which is why she agreed to come. Her work – and to me this has been one of the great illuminations of life – her work itself is a sort of confutation of all the calculations behind this humanistic, scientific view of the world, of life, which the media and other influences are foisting upon our Western people. She considers it worthwhile to go to infinite trouble to bring a dying man in from the street in order that perhaps only for five minutes he may see a loving Christian face before he finally dies. A procedure which, in scientific terms or humanistic terms, is completely crazy, but which I think increases enormously the beauty and the worthiness of being a human being in this world.

Life, any life, contains in itself the potentialities of all life, and therefore deserves our infinite respect, our infinite love, our infinite care. All ideas that we can get rid of manifestations of life which may be inconvenient or burdensome to us, that we can eliminate from our carnal appetites the consequences of carnality in terms of new life; all these notions are of the devil. They all come from below. They are all from the worst that is in us.

I don't want to close what I've been saying to you tonight leaving the impression with you that I feel pessimistic. Of course, I can see, as anyone must who looks at what's going on in the world, the terrible dangers. Pascal puts it very well, you know. He said that when men try to live without God – which is what, in fact, is happening in the Western world now, men and women are trying to live without God – Pascal says when they do that, there are two inevitable consequences: either they suppose that they are gods themselves and go mad (and we have seen enough of that in our time), or they relapse into mere animality. And of course, what Pascal himself didn't see is that even to say they relapse into animality is a kind of gloss on what truly happens. It is something much worse than animality. It's not losing the sacramental ideal of carnality, of eating, in order to have the mere animal idea, but it is moving from the sacramental notion to the really sick notion of treating something that is by its nature related to this human creativity as itself a pleasure, and a pleasure that we should demand to have.

Now I don't want you to think that in pointing that out I'm merely indulging in pessimism. Because it is not so. It is not possible to love Christ and to love the Christian faith and to see what it has done for Western man in the last two thousand years without feeling full of hope and joy. Not possible. Of course it is possible that the particular civilisation that we belong to can collapse, as others have. Of course it is possible that what is called Christendom can come to an end. But Christ can't come to an end. And when we look around, even in this sombre world of today, we have to notice one enormously hopeful thing. And that is, that the efforts to create this world without God, whether through the means of shaping men and controlling men and moulding men into a particular sort of human being, as the Communists have sought to do, or by the mere acceptance of libertinism, of self-indulgence, as Western people have sought to do, in both cases, have proved a colossal failure. From Communist countries we had the voice of someone like Solzhenitsyn. In his recent speech at Harvard, which was a marvellous speech, he said that out of the great suffering of the Russian people would come some new great hope and understanding that the world lacked.

And that out of the very failure of our efforts in the West to escape from the reality of God by the absurdities of affluence, we might expect men to recover their sense of what is real and to escape from a world of fantasy.

You know, it is a funny thing. When you are old there is something that happens that I find very delightful. You often wake up about half past two or three in the morning when the world is very quiet and, in a way, very beautiful. And you feel half in and half out of your body. As though it is really a toss-up whether you go back into that battered old carcase that you can actually see between the sheets, or make off to where you see in the sky, as it were, like the glow of a distant city, what I can only describe as Augustine's City of God. It is a strange thing, but you are aware of these two things: of the old battered carcase and your life in it and this wonderful making off. And at that moment, in that sort of limbo between those two things you have an extraordinarily clear perception of life and everything. And what you realise with a certainty and a sharpness that I can't convey to you is first of all, how extraordinarily beautiful the world is; how wonderful is the privilege of being allowed to live in it, as part of this human experience; of how beautiful the shapes and sounds and colours of the world are; of how beautiful is human love and human work, and all the joys of being a man or a woman in the world. And at the same time, with that, a certainty past any word that I could pass to you, that as a man, a creature, an infinitesimal part of God's creation, you participate in God's purposes for his creation. And that whatever may happen, whatever men may do or not do, whatever crazy projects they may have and lend themselves to, those purposes of God are loving and not hating. Are creative and not destructive. Are universal and not particular. And in that awareness, great comfort and great joy.

This lecture was delivered at the Canberra Theatre, Australia, on October 7th, 1976, being the third Olivier Beguin Memorial Lecture.

The Bible Today

> For the Word of God is quick and powerful, and sharper than any two-edged sword, piercing even to the dividing asunder of soul and spirit, and of the joints and marrow, and is a discerner of the thoughts and intents of the heart.
>
> Epistle to the Hebrews 4:12

WHY THE BIBLE

I have a vivid memory of how, when I was very young – at most in my early teens – I was taken by my father to some sort of Fabian Society gathering to be addressed by H.G. Wells, and of hearing him in that high squeaky voice of his insisting that we just haven't got time to occupy ourselves with the largely mythological doings of an obscure, quarrelsome nomadic tribe like the Israelites. He was referring, of course, to the Bible, and specifically to the Old Testament. Nowadays, such an observation would pass quite unnoticed, humanistic scepticism having moved on to far wilder essays in unbelief than Wells's insistence on his inability to find time for reading and studying the Bible. Then, however, it still seemed delightfully audacious, not to say cheeky, and the little man was obviously well pleased with the notion that he was far too occupied with matters of high import, with writing and speculation of the utmost significance for the future of mankind, to bother his head about such antideluvian trivia as the Garden of Eden, the rise and fall of tinpot monarchs like Saul and David, and the ranting of Hebrew prophets like Jeremiah and Isaiah.

His audience were also well pleased; their faces wore that look of quiet, amused appreciation with which the intelligentsia were wont in those days to respond to any denigration of traditional Christian attitudes. I, too, in so far as I may be said to have thought about the matter at all, was very much of their way of thinking, having been brought up to accept agnosticism if not straight atheism, as the appropriate twentieth century response of an enlightened mind to the Christian religion and its scriptures. For a time I even attended a Socialist Sunday School, but all I can remember about it now is that, though like other Sunday Schools we had hymns and a collection, the discourse to which we were subjected scrupulously avoided any reference to a deity. It goes without saying that there were no prayers, but only the expression of confident hope that under Socialism there would be peace, freedom and brotherhood, in support of which our readings were taken, not from the Bible, but from words of socialist peity like William Morris's *News from Nowhere,* Edward Carpenter's *Towards Democracy,* with occasional forays into Walt Whitman's *Leaves of Grass.* Later, without ostensibly relinquishing this position, well defined by G.K. Chesterton as atheism tempered by hymns, I came to see Wells himself as a sort of clown of the age of science, as, for instance, Cervante's Don Quixote was of the age of chivalry, and Voltaire's Candide of the age of enlightenment; and the more aware I became of the things Wells did find time for, the more perfectly he seemed to fit into the role of being his own Mr Polly, or, in the vein of *The Diary of a Nobody* – one of the few funny works ever to be published by *Punch* – a Mr Pooter of the laboratories.

It is ironical now to reflect that this ribald aspect of Wells alone gives him whatever importance he still has. Clowns and mystics have the special destiny of carrying everything to its ultimate extreme, in the one case of absurdity, in the other of sublimity, bearing the same relation to one another as gargoyles do to steeples. Wells in his gargoyle capacity lives on when the science and scientists he so ardently admired and emulated are in process of being discredited and forgotten. What a wonderful example of Blake's Fearful Symmetry it is that, right at the end of his life, in 1945, when the atomic bomb made its debut on the world's stage, he should have finally turned his face to the wall, in his last book, *Mind at the End of its Tether,* proclaiming despairingly that "the end of everything we call life is close at hand and cannot be evaded .... It is as if everything was driving anyhow to anywhere at a steadily increasing velocity!" So the famous popular prophet of science died in black despair over one of science's greatest achievements – nuclear fission. Truly, God is not mocked. I like very much his description of the breakdown of a technological society – everything driving anyhow to anywhere at a steadily increasing velocity. Horace Walpole produced an eighteenth-century variation on the same theme when he wrote in his *Journal:* "Everything seems to be at sea except the Fleet."

More than ever valid

As I considered preparing this lecture in commemoration of a great Bible-lover, Olivier Beguin, and under the auspices of the Bible Society he did so much to promote, it seemed to me that my purpose must be to, as it were, shout back at Wells across the intervening sixty years or so, that now, contrary to the opinion he had expressed, we desperately need the insights and lessons conveyed by that ancient history of the Jewish people he so disparaged, as it has miraculously come down to us in the splendid vesture of our Authorised Version. Furthermore, that were our present follies and confusions to result in the total destruction of what we still call Western Civilisation, so that no trace remained of its literature, art and learning – a perfectly clear possibility today – and were, centuries later, a copy of our English Bible to be discovered in a Dead Sea cave like the famous Scrolls, and then deciphered, it would still, we may be sure, uplift and enchant its discoverers as it has successive generations of Christians. As for the pursuits and speculations which Wells considered to be so urgent and important that they quite ruled out the Bible as an irrelevant archaism – I mean the quest for power to institute an earthly paradise, for affluence to make it easeful and prosperous, for knowledge to enlarge the citizenry's understanding, and happiness, or, more accurately, pleasures of one sort and another, to keep them in a state of bemused contentment – these, surely, are now as a cul-de-sac into which we have been led, and from which there would seem to be, in earthly terms, no means of egress. In such a case, far from appearing irrelevant, the history of the Children of Israel as recounted in the Old Testament seems more closely related than ever to our own, as the sublime hope of deliverance proclaimed in the New Testament seems more than ever requisite.

If I were to dwell just upon the part the Bible has played in the development and enrichment of our English letters, what it has meant to individual men and women in the way of dedication and inspiration, the manner in which it is inextricably intertwined with out imagery, our values, our ethical and legal systems – or what remains of them – I should easily exhaust my time on just this one theme. A Ukrainian pastor and true servant of Christ showed me once a whole Bible which had been beautifully and meticulously copied out by some of his compatriots to serve in their clandestine worship. I thought of these secret believers toiling away night after night at their task, and reflected that in all history there was no other written matter whose reproduction by such arduous means and in such hazardous circumstances could conceivably have seemed worthwhile. Would similar risks have been taken

adjusted, it can be processed ready for all-purpose use. Thus, geological remains confute the Book of Genesis; a skull found in the Kenyan Highlands proves that creation is older than God, and, with the help of a Teilhard de Chardin, a place can be found for the Ancient of Days a few rungs above *homo sapiens* on the evolutionary ladder.

Procedures for exploring the public mind, opinion polls and such like, we are given to understand, indicate that the number of people who believe that the Bible is true is steadily diminishing, even though each new version continues to sell in hundreds of thousands, and sometimes millions, of copies. Half a century in the communications business has served to intensify my scepticism about procedures which purport to measure statistically individual and social attitudes, and I have long considered that the Romans were more sensible in using the entrails of a chicken rather than a slide-rule to forecast the future. Perhaps the ideal thing would be to use Dr Gallup's entrails, which would have the additional advantage that they could only be used once. Be that as it may, there would seem to be little doubt that of late a continuing process of eroding the Bible's credibility has been taking place, which is doubtless not unconnected with the announcement some years ago by a number of eminent theologians, that God had died – a discovery, incidentally, earlier announced by Nietzsche shortly before repairing to the madhouse in Venice where he was to end his days.

After all, it follows that if God really has died, then the Bible, His Word, must likewise be considered as, if not dead, then decidedly moribund. Its authority, admittedly, was for many centuries unquestionably accepted, not just by run-of-the-mill Christians, but by the most erudite, perceptive and inspired minds of the time. Now we are asked to conclude that, with the coming of the twentieth century, and the immense achievements in it in the way of exploring the phenomena and mechanisms of life, the old believing attitude towards the Bible has become ridiculous. Twentieth century men and women think they know better than their forebears, and dismiss with contumely what scholastics like Thomas Aquinas devoted their lives to studying, and a Blaise Pascal saw as one of the great realities in a world given over to the pursuit of fantasy; what a Michaelangelo and a Leonardo da Vinci portrayed with such frenetic industry and inspiration, and a William Blake, a Johann Sebastian Bach and a Feodor Dostoevsky found to be a major source of illumination; what a Tolstoy was ready, not just to accept as uniquely true, but as providing unique insights into the nature of Man, his earthly existence and heavenly prospects – insights which he wove into the very texture of his thought and writing.

Our credulous era

Personally, I find it on any showing quite ludicrous to suppose that, for nineteen of Christendom's twenty centuries, Christians were credulous idiots ready to believe any tomfoolery the Bible fostered, and that then, with the coming of Darwinism and all that followed therefrom, the scales fell from their eyes, and they realised that the Biblical truths they had been induced to accept were largely fraudulent and absurd. For one thing, it would seem to me that our twentieth century, far from being notable for scientific scepticism, is one of the most credulous eras in all history. It is not that people believe in nothing – which would be bad enough – but that they believe in anything – which is really terrible. Recoiling, as they do, from accepting the validity of miracles, and priding themselves on seeing the Incarnation as a transcendental con-trick, they will accept at its face value any proposition, however nonsensical, that is presented in scientific or sociological jargon – for instance, the existence of a population explosion, which has been so expertly and decisively demolished by Professor Colin Clark of Monash University. Could any mediaeval schoolman, I ask myself, sit through a universally applauded television series like Bronowski's "Ascent of Man" without a smile of derision at such infantile acceptance of unproven and unprovable assertions? Not to mention television advertisements, on a basis of which the most expensively educated populations in the western world alter their dietary and sartorial habits, puff happily at lethal cigarettes recommended as being conducive to romantic encounters by burbling waterfalls or on golden beaches washed by azure seas, and generally follow every whim and fancy wished upon them by the tellymasters.

The difference

Wherein, then, I asked myself in one of those decisive moments which arise all unexpectedly and fatefully as one struggles to break out from the cocoon of fantasy and fly away into the glorious freedom of reality – wherein lies the difference between, say, a Pascal putting aside all his learning, all his egotistic originality, all his pride, and meekly accepting the Bible as God's very Word, and some campus or media pundit scornfully dismissing any such notion as inadmissibly obscurantist and outmoded? The answer came to me, clear, and in a single word – the word "faith" as defined in the Epistle to the Hebrews: "The substance of things hoped for, the evidence of things not seen ." Then I understood on the one hand, truth in terms of faith, as it has shone through the Christian centuries, irradiating everything and everyone; on the other, today's truth in terms of historicity, of fact and circumstance, of clocks ticking out eternity and infinity burgeoning as the millions of light-years expand into milliards. It is the difference between Milton's *Paradise Lost* and Marx's paradise-to-be; between truth which is all-embracing, and meaning which is analytical – as it might be between a body with its flesh and muscles and veins and arteries, a body glorious in its life and fecundity, and an anatomical representation of a body, showing the skeletal structure, the alimentary, bronchial and reproductive systems, all perfectly accurate, except that it isn't a body but a diagram.

In short, it is the difference between how the Bible presented itself to a St Augustine or a Dr Johnson, and how it has presented itself to its contemporary expounders – an Albert Schweitzer, a Rudolf Bultmann.

One of the most difficult things in the world to express in words, with their inexorable limitation of having a beginning and an ending, is the revelation of truth as a totality, in contradistinction to the current quest for truth in terms of particularities, of meaning merely. The greatest and most articulate mystics admit their inability to describe the moment when faith takes possession of heart and mind, and the particularities of belief become insignificant, and even irrelevant, by comparison with the sense of oneness that faith has inculcated. Just as, the moment one truly loves, it is totally, with no reference to particularities of body or mind, so, in loving God, one glimpse of His presence, and then every blemish, all sin and affliction, all that tarnishes and confuses our mortal existence, is incorporated in the great proposition of love on which our earth, ourselves and all creation, animate or inanimate, is founded.

Futile disputation

In the light of this illumination I understand that all the disputation that has raged in recent years as to whether an historical Jesus can be constructed out of the Biblical one, as to the precise meaning of the Bible's words as distinct from what they have conveyed to generations of Christians literate and illiterate, sophisticated and simple, celebrated and nonentities – that all this disputation has been utterly sterile and futile, the terrible pedantry of unbelievers desperately trying to put together with their intellects the debris of a shattered faith. As C.S. Lewis indicates in his incomparable *Screwtape Letters* it is a favourite device of the Devil to set people wrangling about inessentials in order to take their mind off essentials, which he then filches – a practice also favoured by pickpockets and politicians.

Either the Bible is veritably the Word of God, or it is merely another *Iliad.* only about the Jewish people rather than the classical Greeks; just as Jesus is either the Son of God, as he claimed, or one more exalté knocking around in Galilee during the Roman occupation when such types proliferated there. If the Bible is merely a very fine book, and Jesus no more than a very fine man, then Christianity is, at best, an exhibit in a museum of world religions, and the Bible a haphazard collection of legendary writings, of interest, maybe, to anthropologists and other specialists, but of little or no help in enabling people to shape up to the experience of being mortal while prone to intimations of immortality, of being intrinsically imperfect, yet capable of conceiving and aspiring after perfection.

In this connection, there are two sayings of Blake that I have found particularly relevant to the question of the truth or authenticity of the Bible. "Truth," he wrote, "can never be told so as to be understood and not be believed," and: "Everything possible to be believed is an image of truth." In a similar vein, he distinguishes between seeing with and through the eye:

> This Life's dim windows of the Soul
> Distorts the Heavens from Pole to Pole
> And leads you to believe a Lie
> When you see with not thro', the eye.

Seen with the eye, the Biblical accounts of, for instance, the creation, and of Jesus' birth, ministry, death and resurrection seem hopelessly at odds with the factual criteria which science has imposed for distinguishing between accuracy and inaccuracy. Seen through the eye, however, the factual criteria no longer apply, any more than they do when Shakespeare sets one of his scenes on a non-existent seaboard in Bohemia. Christian believers fashioned their beliefs into an image of truth, making it understandable, and therefore, believable, whereas the nonbelievers of an age of science, having no beliefs, have no recourse but to plump for facts, and so are stuck with statistics and computers to mass-produce them. So much data! So little faith! Verily those that take to statistics shall perish through statistics.

Similarly with history, which shapes and colours our myths, as myths in their turn reveal the true nature of history. In this sense, as Tolstoy insists, there is no such thing as "true" history, only a series of fluctuating visions, whereas myths express the everlasting reality of which history is the ever-changing shadow. Seen through rather than with the eye, the Fearful Symmetry (another Blakean expression) declares itself – that in trying to construct perfection in their own image, to set up an earthly paradise, men only succeed in underlining their own imperfection, so that their earthly paradise invariably becomes a heavenly hell. Seeking happiness, they fall into despair, seeking knowledge, into obscurantism and credulity, seeking freedom, into total servitude, and seeking security, into total vulnerability. We may rejoice that it should be so, this being God's way of ensuring that, however far we stray, we can never be finally lost; that however dense the darkness, at the heart of it a light shines. This is the essential message of the Bible, itself a protracted and stupendous exercise in seeing through the eye.

THE RELEVANCE OF THE BIBLE TODAY

It may be doubted whether many people read the Bible today, as was once the widespread practice. Except in specially pious homes, there is no family reading, and the habit of a daily portion, whether as prescribed in the *Book of Common Prayer* or in collections like *Daily Light,* is fast disappearing. Yet, as I have found, there is no more uplifting and stimulating way of beginning a day. The metaphysical poets, especially George Herbert, are quite magical in their power to deflect one's spirit from sordid or carnal preoccupations, as are great mystical works like *The Cloud of Unknowing,* but nothing can compare with the Bible itself in its power to reveal in the ramshackle edifice of Time a window looking out onto a vista of Eternity, all bathed in the bright light of God's universal love. The anxiety, depression and despair liable to afflict us all, perhaps particularly nowadays, are a factor of the Ego, and it is remarkable how they are dispersed by the words of the Bible – as, the beautiful poetry of the Psalms, the power and majesty of Isaiah, the sheer narrative skill of the story of Job and Jonah, the tremendous drama of David's life, and the sayings of those truly inspired men, the Hebrew prophets.

Ultimate relevance

But, of course for Christians the ultimate relevance of the Bible lies in the New Testament, in its account of the Incarnation and all the momentous sequel. We and the Incarnation stand or fall together; to abandon or repudiate its circumstances and consequences as set forth in the New Testament is tantamount to tearing up the title deeds of a property, and inviting in the squatters and the demolition men.

One of the many pleasures of old age is the realisation it brings that there is no possibility of reconstructing the past as it actually was. This is particularly the case for those like myself whose occupation has been what St Augustine called vendors of words, or, in contemporary parlance, journalism. It quite often happens that I get some book to review, or have occasion to look at some documentary film footage, purporting to convey happenings in which I was professionally involved – as, for instance, the economic depression in the late 'twenties and early 'thirties, or the famine in the USSR at the time of Stalin's collectivisation of agriculture, or the London Blitz, or the so-called Liberation of Paris. Invariably it turns out that these exercises in actuality, in the light of my own experience strike me as being off-beam – cinema falsité rather than verité. In other words, there is no possibility of producing definitive, objective history; the vast amount of documentary material that exists is, by its nature, all slanted and subjective, and gets assembled according to the prejudices and preconceptions of the assembler, or historian, in the light of the prevailing consensus, or zeitgeist, and so is subject to revision at the hands of other historians operating in the atmosphere of another zeitgeist.

Basis of history

Thus, when I was first in India in 1924, schoolchildren were being taught that their country was in a sorry state until the happy day when the Sahibs landed on their shores and established the British Raj. Thereafter, the people had enjoyed stability, law and order and other intimations of collective well-being. Nowadays, they are being taught that India was in a sorry state until the Sahibs were kicked out, when their country entered upon a new era of peace and prosperity. No doubt before very long they will be being taught that Mrs Gandhi, that well-known running-dog of capitalist imperialism, brought their country to the verge of ruin, but then the Communists took over, and it has been steadily getting better and better ever since. These historical propositions, it goes without saying, are equally spurious, and merely express what is the basis of all history – the propaganda of the victor.

The Bible considered as history is likewise the propaganda of the victor, but in its case the victor in question is unique in being, not a man, or men, or an ideal, or a cause, but God Himself. This is what makes the Bible different in kind from all other historical works. The world changes, and a detached, agnostic eighteenth century view such as suffuses Gibbon's *Decline and Fall of the Roman Empire,* becomes obsolete. A liberal view like G.M. Trevelyan's likewise loses its relevance; as does an increasingly pessimistic humanist view like Arnold Toynbee's, and a Marxist view like Christopher Hill's. The Bible's account of the history of the Children of Israel, on the other hand, and of how the good news of Jesus' Kingdom was proclaimed and received, deals rather with Man's relationship to God than with the doings of men, and so is not susceptible to what King Lear in his affliction called "the rise and fall of great ones that ebb and flow with the moon." The works of historians, from Thucydides onwards, similarly ebb and flow with the moon, but the Bible, precisely because its gaze is fixed on God rather than men, on truth rather than happenings, on the constant force of love rather than the fluctuations of power, can never become outmoded or irrelevant. So, our approach to the Bible must be like Milton's to the great task he had set himself in *Paradise Lost*, in humility, in reverence, in dedication:

> What in me is dark
> Illumine, what is low raise and support;
> That to the height of this great argument
> I may assert eternal Providence
> And justify the ways of God to men.

THE FUTURE OF THE BIBLE

As it happens, we are living in one of those periods when the only certainty is uncertainty, and the only sure prospect the absence of any sure prospect. It is quite possible, if not probable, that many of my present listeners will live to see the final disintegration of our western civilisation: and as part of that process our religious institutions and their affiliates are likely to share the fate of secular institutions – our parliaments, our law courts, our universities, so that an Olivier Beguin of the future may well find himself producing and circulating clandestine Bibles, perhaps written out by hand like my Ukrainian friend's. There are many indications that this total dissolution of our present way of life is not something that is going to happen, but that is already happening. During the London Blitz I had a strange sense that the buildings on fire and collapsing were already in ruins before the bombs fell, as the walls of Jericho were already crumbling when Joshua's trumpet sounded. In the same sort of way, it is difficult to resist the conclusion that there is a death-wish at work at the heart of our civilisation whereby our bankers promote the inflation which will ruin them, our educationalists seek to create the moral and intellectual chaos which will nullify their professional purposes, our physicians invent new and more terrible diseases to replace those they have abolished, our moralists cut away the roots of all morality and our theologians systematically dismantle the structure of belief they exist to expound and promote. Certainly, it is difficult to think of anything professional subversives, anarchists and atheists have attempted which is not being better done by the ostensible guardians of our laws, our constitutional liberties and our religious faith.

Yet if it is the case that the Bible contains words of everlasting truth, then those words must stand whatever may happen to us and our world. As Jesus himself said: "Heaven and earth shall pass away, but my words shall not pass away." I think of Augustine when, in his fifty-seventh year, the news was brought to him that Rome had fallen. In worldly terms, it was a dire catastrophe; confronted with it, Augustine turned his thoughts away from the earthly city which had meant so much to him, and towards the City of God. This is a City, he said, which, unlike their earthly ones, men did not build, and which men cannot destroy. What I have been trying, very inadequately, to say is that the Bible is its book.

Comrade or Brother!

There is a vast, but often unnoticed, difference between the political concept of equality and the Christian concept of brotherhood. The fact is that men are not on any showing equal, but they are brothers. To pretend that they are equal results, as all fantasies do, in demonstrating the opposite – their inexorable inequality. Thus, the *egalité* of the French Revolution led to Napoleon and the Third Republic, both particularly vulgar exercises in inequality. Similarly, the allegedly 'self-evident' truth in the American Declaration of Independence, that all men are created equal, has led to a society which easily accepted the institution of slavery, and to this day tolerates, and even glorifies, disparities in wealth more excessive than in any other western country. As for the Russian Revolution, it would be necessary to go back to the Great Moguls and the Peacock Throne to find a parallel to the sycophantic adulation that Stalin, and to a somewhat lesser degree his successors, have considered to be their due. Whatever else may be said of the way of life the Revolution has brought about, it cannot by any stretch of the imagination be called egalitarian. As Solzhenitsyn has pointed out – and he speaks from personal experience – only in the lower depths of the Gulag Archipelago is there any true equality between man and man, and in our decidedly rundown British welfare state, purportedly based on the principle of equality, envy, rancour, class-consciousness and other intimations of a sense of inequality are as much in evidence as ever before in our history, if not more so.

Christian brotherhood, on the other hand, presupposes a family, all of whose members deserve equal consideration. A mother knows perfectly well that her children are unequal – one beautiful and another plain, one bright and another slow-witted, one strong and another sickly; maybe one who is 'simple', or, in contemporary phraseology, 'mentally handicapped'. Does she differentiate between them? Not at all. Or if she does, more often than not it is in favour of the weaker, the plainer, the slower-witted, the handicapped one. A mongol child is often greatly beloved. At Lourdes, when I was there to do the commentary for a television programme, I made the acquaintance of an elderly lady who had brought her grown-up son with her. He had been unable to sit up from birth, but looking after him was the joy of her life, and her only dread that he might be sent away to an institution.

So it is with God, the father of our human family, who, we are told, cares so much about his creatures that he has counted the hairs of each separate individual head, and cannot see even a sparrow fall to the ground without concern. Thus every single human being, whatever his condition or circumstances, is equally precious in God's eyes, and deserving of the same consideration. It follows that, in Christian terms, no one human being can ever be regarded as intrinsically in an inferior category to another. Hence the fallacy and abomination of the doctrine of apartheid in South Africa. If, as members of God's family, we are equally beloved of Him, then surely we are required so to regard one another.

It is true, of course, that, through the centuries of Christendom, Christians have not managed to live up to this concept, though the Christian mystics have celebrated it, and the saints like St Francis have practised it; as, for instance, does Mother Teresa today. Nonetheless, there have been monstrous infringements, particularly on the part of states, governments, churches and other such institutions, and of individuals associated with them. Yet the notion of all men equally dear to their creator, and therefore to one another, has survived, providing the basis for whatever is just in our justice, moral in our *mores,* equitable in our way of life; above all, for the concept of human freedom and human rights about which there has been so much talk of late. Abolish that notion, and western man will discover in bitterness and tears that without it he has no freedom, nor any rights.

This is what the Grand Inquisitor and the returned Christ are talking about in the famous scene in Dostoevsky's novel *The Brothers Karamazov* when they confront one another in sixteenth-century Seville. The Grand Inquisitor explains that the freedom Christ brought into the world on his previous visitation has proved intolerable, and that therefore if He insists on returning and reviving it, He will have to suffer the same fate as any other dangerous heretic and again be executed. Equality, likewise, belongs to Christ's kingdom of love, not to the kingdom of power the devil offered Him and that He rejected. It cannot be attained by any law, revolution, or other rearrangement of human authority. Least of all, let me add, can it be attained in laboratories by genetic rearrangement, or in the abortion and euthanasia abattoirs.

Through having a face that, because of television, is liable to be recognised, and being known nowadays as someone who takes a Christian position, people quite often come up to me and by one means or another indicate that they, too, are Christians. Thus, when I am leaving a restaurant, a waiter silently pads after me, not, as I thought might be the case, to complain about his tip, but to shake my hand as a fellow-Christian. Or in – of all places – a make-up room the girl attending to my ancient battered visage whispers in my ear: "I love the Lord!" Or, turning a corner, I come face to face with a West Indian, who, with an enormous grin of recognition, shouts out: "Dear brother in Christ!" Or an air-hostess, stooping down to arrange my seat, murmers that, for her too, Christ is all in all.

These encounters are altogether delightful, but there is more to it than that. Note that it never for a moment occurs to me to want to know whether these diverse people who greet me so charmingly are educated or uneducated, bourgeois or proletarian, Roman Catholics or Protestants or what have you, what is their IQ, how much they earn or any other such particular. All the different categories we have devised just don't apply. There is but one category – our common fellowship in Christ.

This, it seems to me, is the true image of Christian brotherhood and the quality derived therefrom – workaday encounters glorified by participation in a common lot, as children of the same God, redeemed by the same Saviour, and destined for the same salvation. Marx saw the apogee of our mortal existence in a victorious proletariat living happily ever after in a society whose government has withered away; Bunyan saw us as pilgrims making our way as best we might to the City of God where we belong. I am for Bunyan.

Anatomy of Sainthood

Along with a vast multitude of people all over the world, I rejoiced over the award of the Nobel Peace Prize to Mother Teresa. Not, obviously, because the award, as such, enhanced her, though she may well have enhanced the award; funded, as it is, by conscience money provided by the inventor of dynamite. After all, previous recipients were the Prime Minister of North Vietnam and Dr Kissinger; not exactly doves of peace, I should have thought. No, the glory of the award was precisely the glow of satisfaction it gave to all of us who love and respect Mother Teresa, in the knowledge that it would serve to spread yet further afield awareness of the ministry of love and compassion in which she and her Missionaries of Charity are so valiantly engaged.

When I first set eyes on her, which is now some fifteen years ago – the occasion was a casual TV interview – I at once realised that I was in the presence of someone of unique quality. This was not due to her appearance, which is homely and unassuming, so that words like 'charm' or 'charisma' do not apply. Nor to her shrewdness and quick understanding, though these are very marked; nor even to her manifest piety and true humility and ready laughter. There is a phrase in one of the psalms that always, for me, evokes her presence: 'the beauty of holiness' – that special beauty, amounting to a kind of pervasive luminosity generated by a life dedicated wholly to loving God and His creation. This, I imagine, is what the haloes in Mediaeval paintings of saints were intended to convey.

Thinking about Mother Teresa, as I often do, and realising that by all the odds she will one day be canonised, I try to sort out the various characteristics in her of a saint. First of all, contrary to what might be supposed, other-worldliness is not one of them. Mother Teresa is very firmly settled here on earth, in time and in mortality, and her judgements relating thereto have proved to be quite remarkably shrewd and perceptive. Her practicality never ceases to amaze me. Thus, she is responsible for some two hundred and forty houses in different parts of the world, including some in places like the Yemen and Zagreb which present particular hazards. The headquarters of a business of comparable size and distribution would occupy a whole skyscraper, filled with managerial staff, computers, secretaries, tape-machines and teleprinters tapping away.

Mother Teresa manages without any of this plant and paraphernalia, dealing with her correspondence in her own hand, usually late at night, and travelling about the world in the most economical way possible. At one point she offered herself as an air hostess to Air India in return for free travel. Alas, the offer was not accepted, but what an air hostess she would have made! Money that comes in is exclusively for the poor, not for administration; in any case, she assumes, it will turn up as and when required. And so, miraculously, it does. She has even forbidden her co-workers to organise fund-rasing campaigns, which, she insists, distract their attention from their true work of comforting and helping the lonely, the afflicted and the despairing.

On the one hand, she makes mystical concepts seem an integral part of day-to-day living; on the other, she, as it were, transcendentalises our most ordinary conclusions and expectations. Thus, she persuades aspiring helpers who are too incapacitated to become active members of her order, that somehow or other their fortitude in accepting their affliction gives her additional strength and courage for her work; that their endurance of suffering is her powerhouse. I have myself seen a lady preparing to undergo her umpteenth operation all shining and joyful because she is convinced that thereby Mother Teresa will acquire extra muscle in the service of Christ. At the same time, she managed to induce high caste Indian ladies to minister to derelicts brought in from the streets of Calcutta – something that, as someone who has lived, one way and another, a number of years in India, I should never have believed possible.

Her response to happenings and circumstances is always so wonderfully apt. For instance, to the Peace Prize award, to disappear for a month into a strict retreat, leaving the cameramen and interviewers to disperse, the telephone calls and letters and telegrams unanswered. Or, while waiting to be interviewed on a coast-to-coast American TV talk show, and noting that advertisement after advertisement was of packaged food recommended as being non-fattening and non-nourishing, to remark, quietly but audibly: "I see that Christ is needed in television studios."

Of course, she enjoys the inestimable advantage of never looking at TV, listening to radio or reading the newspapers, and so has a clear notion of what is really going on in the world; the siren-voice of the consensus does not reach her. This enables her to post her Missionaries of Charity about the world so as to be exactly where they are most needed. Like St Francis with his friars, she expects them to carry laughter with them as well as charity; like an earlier St Theresa – of Avila, but Mother Teresa always carefully explains that she is named after the little one, of Lisieux – in her standing orders, she does not overrate what this world has to offer.

The order she has founded is, I should suppose, as strict as any now in existence, if not stricter. Yet, though, in orders that have softened the rigours of their rule, novices are few and far between, Mother Teresa's is bombarded by girls asking to enter. Some time ago she came to visit me with some twenty-five of these aspiring Missionaries of Charity, of numerous races and nations, and all, as it seemed to me, enchanting in their eagerness to join Mother Teresa, and obvious delight at being accepted to share a life whose ardours contrast so sharply with the self-indulgence considered today to be synonymous with happiness and 'quality of life'. How curious that others seem not to understand, what is so clear to her, that the more that is asked on Christ's behalf, the more that will be accorded, and vice versa!

I could go on and on enumerating the saintly qualities in Mother Teresa, but however many I listed, they would not add up to sainthood, which is something else. Jean-Pierre de Caussade writes of how all the time the sequel to the New Testament is being written by saintly souls in the succession of the prophets and apostles, not in canonical books, but by continuing the history of divine purpose with their lives. So, just as great artists have painted the Incarnation, great writers described and dramatised it, great composers set it to music, great architects built it, great saints live it, by Mother Teresa's mere presence, even just by thinking about her, the follies and confusions of our time are confuted. This is what saints are for; you spell them out, and lo! the Holy Spirit has spoken.

The True Crisis of Our Time

It would be difficult for anyone looking around the world today to resist the conclusion that something has gone wrong very badly indeed with what we continue to call western civilisation. This awareness tends to be distorted and muffled, if not obliterated, by the media which manage to induce us to take for granted the continuingly explosive situations that confront us on every hand and to see as an enlargement of our freedom and an enhancement of the quality of our living the steady and ominous erosion of the moral standards of which our traditional way of life has been based.

Regarding the reversal of moral standards, so that as the horrid sisters chant in Macbeth "Fair is foul and foul is fair," there are some words by Simone Weil – I don't know whether you are familiar with her – a French Jewess who was also a lady of great mystical insight, who actually died in this country in the war. Simone Weil's luminous intelligence and insights are among the most penetrating of our time, which bear very clearly on this not just confusion between the concepts of good and evil but the actual replacement of one by the other. "Nothing is so beautiful," she writes, "nothing is so continually fresh and surprising, so full of sweet and perpetual ecstasy as the good. No deserts are so dreary, monotonous and boring as evil. But with fantasy it is the other way round. Fictional good is boring and flat, while fictional evil is varied, intriguing attractive and full of charm."

Let me turn also, in a similar theme, to Pascal, who in his *Pensées* says this: "It is in vain O men that you seek within yourselves the cure of all your miseries. All your insight only leads you to the knowledge that it is not in yourselves that you will discover the true and the good. The philosophers promise them to you and have not been able to keep their promise. Your principle maladies are pride which cut you off from God; sensuality which binds you to the earth; and they have done nothing but foster at least one of these maladies. If they have given you God for your object it has only been to pander to your pride. They have made you think that you were like Him and resembled Him by your nature and those who have grasped the vanity of such a pretension have cast you down into the other abyss by making you believe that your nature was like that of the beasts of the field and have led you to seek your good in lust which is the lot of animals." In other words egomania and erotomania: the two ills of our time, the raised fist and the raised phallus.

Let us also turn, in our imagination, to Carthage in the year 410 when St Augustine received the news that Rome, the great Rome, had been sacked and the barbarians had taken over. His first thought is to reassure his flock: "If this catastrophe is indeed true," he tells them, "it must be God's will. Men build cities and men destroy cities but the city of God they didn't build and cannot destroy. The heavenly city," he goes on "outshines Rome beyond comparison. There instead of victory is truth; instead of high rank, holiness; instead of peace, felicity; instead of life, eternity. There take Aristotle; put him near to the rock of Christ and he fades away into nothingness. Who is Aristotle when he hears the words Christ said then he shakes in hell? Pythagoras said this, Plato said that. Put them near the Rock and compare these arrogant people with him who was crucified. Thus we come to see that in our fallen state, our imperfection, we can conceive perfection. Through the Incarnation, the presence of God among us and the lineaments of man we have a window in the walls of time which looks out onto this heavenly city." This was Augustine's profoundest conclusion which in his great work, he enshrined imperishably to be a comfort, and a light in the dark days that lay ahead. In the year 430, the triumphant vandals would come into Africa reaching the walls of Hippo itself as its Bishop Augustine lay dying there. Today the earthly city looks ever larger to the point where it may be said to have taken over the heavenly one turning away from God. Blown up with the arrogance generated by their fabulous success in exploring and harnessing the mechanism of life, men believe themselves at least in charge of their own destiny. As we survey the disastrous consequences of such an attitude, the chaos and destruction it has brought, as Augustine did the fall of Rome and its aftermath, his word on that other occasion still stands applicable as he says to all circumstances and conditions of men.

In the past too, of course, other efforts have been made to demolish Christianity in the name of superior knowledge and political wisdom. Blake, in his inimitable way deals faithfully with such efforts. He writes, "Mock on, mock on, Voltaire, Rousseau, Rock on, rock on, 'tis all in vain. You throw the sand against the wind. And the wind blows it back again." Of course, Simone Weil wrote the words that I read well before television had been developed, in due course to attract huge audiences all over the world, becoming incomparably the greatest fabricator and purveyor of fantasy that has ever existed and occupying the attention of the average adult in the Western world for some thirty-five hours a week or twelve years of the three score years and ten of a normal lifespan. It's an amazing thought, especially when one considers what appears on the TV screen, that so large a proportion of a lifespan should be devoted to staring into it. Its only merit, in my opinion, is that it has a splendidly soporific effect. It is not uncommon to see a whole family sleeping quietly round their television set. My own particular nightmare is falling asleep in front of a TV set in the days when I used to appear on television and then coming to suddenly and noting on the screen a figure, seemingly familiar, which turns out to be myself. It is a sort of macabre experience that only Edgar Allan Poe could have done justice to, and gave me a tremendous sense of the appalling danger of trafficking in images, which is what television is about. Shortly after this experience, I decided to give up watching television and have my aerials removed — a painless operation but one that makes you feel much better afterwards. The offerings of television bear out Simone Weil's proposition to a quite remarkable degree, for in them it is almost invariably Eros rather than Agape translated as Charity in that wonderful thirteenth chapter of St Paul's first epistle to the Corinthians that provides all the excitement. Success and celebrity rather than a broken and a contrite heart are made to seem desirable, and Jesus Christ Superstar rather than Jesus Christ on the cross who gets a folk hero's billing.

Television, I should say, in the light of what I know about it — my memories of working with it are the ultimate in fantasy — a sort of Caliban's island full of sounds and sweet airs that give delight and hurt not, so that when we wake, if we ever do, we cry to sleep again; and it is precisely the transportation of good and evil in this world of fantasy that in my opinion lies at the root of our present malaise. Such was also Solzhenitsyn's first impression when he arrived in the West: our troubles, he said, were due precisely to our loss of any awareness of good and evil. It's good and evil. It's good and evil after all that provides the theme of the drama of our mortal existence. In this sense you might capture them with the positive and negative points that generate an electric current. Transpose the points and the current fails, the lights go out, darkness falls and all is confusion. What I wish to put to you here is that the darkness falling on our civilisation is likewise due to a transposition of good and evil. In other words, that we are suffering not from an energy crisis or an over population crisis or an unemployment crisis – from none of these ills that are commonly specified. The root cause of our trouble is that we have lost our sense of a moral order in the universe without which no order whatsoever, economic, social, political is attainable. For Christians of course this moral order is derived from that terrific moment when, as it is so splendidly put in the wisdom of Solomon "while all things were in quiet silence and that night was in the midst of her swift course, thine almighty word leaped down from heaven out of thy royal throne, leaped down to dwell among us full of grace and truth." It was thus that our western civilisation came into existence, deriving not from Darwin's origin of species, not from the Communist manifesto, or even the American Declaration of Independence, but from the great drama of the Incarnation as conveyed in the New Testament. To abandon or repudiate finally this almighty word would assuredly be to wind up inexorably two thousand years of history and ourselves with it. It is true, of course, that my own sense of a world hopelessly lost in fantasy to the point of being quite cut off from its origins, from the true fount of its life and creativity, whether spiritual, moral or even maternal has been heightened by the practice of the profession of journalism. I look back on more than half a century of knock-about journalism comprising pretty well everything in the business – for instance ultra-solemn leading articles tapped out on a typewriter: "The people of this country will never for a moment countenance" – something or other that they are shortly going to countenance with the greatest of ease if not indifference. On *The Guardian*, where I began my vendorship of words, we were supposed to finish up our editorials on a hopeful note so we usually concluded our theme with some bromide like "It's greatly to be hoped that wiser counsels may yet prevail and moderate men of all shades of opinion brought together."

Alas, as I soon discovered, wiser counsels were notably not prevailing and it was immoderate men who were drawing together. Then there were the pontifical despatches hurriedly put together from our special correspondent, here, there and everywhere, and tabloid features on "Why eating yogurt makes men live for ever." The fact is, there is built into life a strong ironical theme for which we should be duly grateful to our Creator, since it helps us to find our way through the fantasy which encompasses us to the reality of our existence – what Blake called its "fearful symmetry". God has mercifully made diversions whereby we seek to evade this reality – I mean the pursuit of power, of sensual delight, of money, of learning, of celebrity, of happiness – so manifestly preposterous that we are forced to turn to Him for help and for mercy. We seek wealth and find we have accumulated only worthless pieces of paper. We seek security and find we have on our hands the means to blow ourselves and our little earth to smithereens. Looking for calm satisfaction we find ourselves involved in sterility rites as looking for freedom we infallibly fall into the servitude of self-gratification. We look back on history and what do we see? Empires rising and falling, revolutions and counter-revolutions succeeding one another, wealth accumulating and wealth dispersed, one nation dominant and then another. As Shakespeare's King Lear puts it, "The rise and fall of great ones that ebb and flow with the moon." In one lifetime I have seen my fellow countrymen ruling over one quarter of the world and the great majority of them convinced in the words of what is still a favourite song, "God has made them mighty and will make them mightier yet." I have heard a crazed Austrian announce the establishment of a German Reich that was to last for a thousand years; an Italian clown report the calendar to begin again with his assumption of power; a murderous Georgian brigand in the Kremlin acclaimed by the intellectual elite as wiser than Solomon, more enlightened than Asoka, more humane than Marcus Aurelius. I have seen

America wealthier than all the rest of the world put together and with the superiority of weaponry that would have enabled Americans, had they so wished, to outdo an Alexander or a Julius Caesar in the range and scale of conquest. All in one little lifetime gone with the wind. England now a part of an island off the coast of Europe threatened with further dismemberment; Hitler and Mussolini seen as buffoons; Stalin a sinister name in the regime he helped to found and dominated totally for three decades; Americans haunted by fears of running out of the precious fluid that keeps their motorways roaring and the smog settling, by memories of a disastrous military campaign in Vietnam and the windmills of Watergate. Can this really be what life is about? The worldwide soap opera going on from century to century, from era to era whose old discarded sets and props litter the earth – surely not. Was it to provide a location for so repetitive and ribald a production as this that the universe was created and man or *homo sapiens* as he likes to call himself, heavens knows why, came into existence. I can't believe it. If this were all, then the cynic, the hedonist and the suicides are right: the most we can hope for from life is amusement, gratification of our senses and death. But it is not all. Thanks to the great mercy and marvel of the Incarnation, the cosmic scene is resolved into a human drama. God reaches down to become a man and man reaches up to relate himself to God. Time looks into eternity and eternity into time making now always and always now. Everything is transformed by this sublime dream of the Incarnation, God's special parable for fallen man in a fallen world. The way opens before us, charted in the birth, ministry, death and resurrection of Jesus Christ: the way that successive generations of believers have striven to follow deriving themselves the moral, spiritual and intellectual creativity out of which have come everything truly great in our art, our literature, our music, the splendour of the great cathedrals and the illumination of the saints and mystics, as well as countless lives of men and women serving their God and loving their Saviour in humility and faith. It is a glorious record, not just of the past but continuing now. The books are open not closed; the Incarnation was not a mere historical event like the battle of Waterloo or the American Declaration of Independence, something that happened and then was over. It goes on happening all the time. God did not retreat back into Heaven when the fateful words "it is finished" were uttered on Golgotha. The Word that became flesh has continued and continues to dwell among us full of grace and truth. There are examples on every hand, we have but to look for them: for instance, the man in Solzhenitsyn's labour camp who scribbled sentences from the gospels that he pulled out of his pocket in the evening to keep himself serene and brotherly in that terrible place. Then Solzhenitsyn himself, a product of this world's first overtly atheistic materialist society, yet can tell us in shining words that "it was only when I lay there on rotting prison straw that I sensed within myself the first stirrings of good. Gradually it was disclosed to me that the line separating good and evil passes not from states nor between classes, nor between political parties either, but right through every human heart and through all human hearts. So bless you, prison, for having been in my life." What insight, what wisdom, acquired in a soviet prison after a Marxist upbringing.

Again there is Mother Teresa and her ever-growing Missionaries of Charity, going about their work of love with their own special geography of compassion moving into country after country. Sisters, now of many nationalities, arriving in twos and threes in the troubled places of this troubled world with nothing to offer except Christ, no other purpose than to see in every suffering man, woman, the person of their Saviour and to heed his words "Insofar as ye did it unto the least of these my brethren ye did it unto me."

If the Christian revelation is true, then it must be true

for all times and in all circumstances, whatever may happen, however seemingly inimicable to it may be the way the world is going, and those who preside over its affairs. Its truth intact and inviolate: "Heaven and earth shall pass away," our Lord said, "but my word shall not pass away." Our western civilisation, like others before it, is subject to decay and some time or other must decompose and disappear. The world's way of responding to intimations of decay is to engage equally in idiot hopes and idiot despair. On the one hand, some new policy or discovery is confidently expected to put everything to rights: a new fuel, a new drug, detente, world government, North Sea oil, revolution or counter-revolution. On the other, some disaster is confidently expected to prove our undoing: Capitalism will break down, Communism won't work, fuel will run out, plutonium will lay us low, atomic waste will kill us all, over-population will suffocate us, alternately a declining birth rate will put us at the mercy of our enemies. In Christian terms, such hopes and fears are equally beside the point. As Christians we know that here we have no continuing city, that crowns roll in the dust and every earthly kingdom must sometime flounder, whereas, with knowledge of a king men did not crown and cannot dethrone, we are citizens of a city man did not build and cannot destroy. Thus the Apostle Paul wrote to the Christians in Rome, living in a society as depraved and dissolute as ours with the TV, the games which specialise as television does in spectacles of violence and eroticism, exhorting them to be steadfast, unmovable, always abounding in God's word, to concern themselves with the things that are not seen. For the things which are seen are temporal, but the things that are not seen are eternal. It was in the breakdown of Rome that Christendom was born and now in the breakdown of Christendom there are the same requirements and the same possibilities to eschew the fantasy of this disintegrating world and seek the reality of what is not seen, an eternal, the reality of Christ. In this reality of Christ we may see our only hope, our only prospect in a darkening world. After all, even if one or other of the twentieth-century nightmare utopias were veritably to come to pass: if men proved capable of constructing their kingdom of heaven on earth with abundance ever broadening down from one gross national product to another, and the motorways reaching from here to eternity and Eros released to begin a regulation two offspring like a well-behaved child at a party taking just two cakes otherwise frolicking in contraceptive bliss, all our genes counted and selected to produce only beauty queens and MENSA IQs, the divergences all thrown away with other waste products and the media providing Musak and Newsak round the clock to delight and inform all and sundry and the appropriate medicaments available to cure all actual and potential ills. It may well be the case that western man has wearied of his freedom and is now consciously or unconsciously engrossed in shedding the burden it imposes on him thereby, if he but knew it, headed inexorably to servitude. Yet in Christ whoever cares to can find freedom, the glorious freedom of the children of God, the only lasting freedom there is. To quote once more St Paul: "Where the spirit of the Lord is, there is liberty." Again, it may well be that western man has turned away from the Cross in favour of an illusory pursuit of happiness, yet if the preaching of the Cross is indeed to them that perish foolishness, to those who believe, it continues to be the power of God whereby affliction is seen as part of his love and out of a public execution burgeoned the most perfect hopes and joys the human heart has ever attained. What then is there to fear or dread? Jean Pierre de Caussade speaks of the sacrament of the present moment: "To surrender ourselves to God's will, not with reference to yesterday or tomorrow, but now, fully, truly, whatever may or may not happen in the world irrespective of the buffooneries of power under whatever demogogue or dictators may be thrown up."

Fortified with this sacrament of the present we may laugh at the confusion of our present civilisation as Rabelais, in the person of Panurge, laughed at the antics of carnal man; as Cervantes, in the person of Don Quixote, laughed at the antics of crusading man; as Shakespeare, in the person of Sir John Flastaff, laughed at the antics of mortal man. It is in the breakdown of power that we may discern its true nature and when power seems strong and firm that we are most liable to be taken in and suppose that it can really be used to enhance human freedom and well-being, forgetful that Jesus is the product of the loser's, not the victor's camp and to proclaim that the first will be last, that the weak are the strong and the fools are the wise.

It was through brooding on the strange phenomena of our time that I came to see in the liberal-minded self intimation of a death wish and to realise that its dominance in the western world, especially since the emergence of the United States as the preponderant influence, and the development of the all-powerful media, for whose fraudulent processes and procedures the liberal mind has a singular aptitude, was responsible for the gaderine bias apparant in all our policies and projects. In other words, there we were confronted, not with a whole series of crises and problems, but with one crisis amounting to a death wish, an urge to self-destruction seeping into every aspect of our way of life especially our values, our beliefs, our aspirations, how we see the past and our hopes for the future, the qualities we cherish and those we hold up to obliquy. A touch of irony is added by virtue of the fact that this gaderine course is associated with ostensibly optimistic views, with the notion of a perfect society or kingdom of heaven on earth attained by human effort; in Marxist terms by the final triumph of the proletariat over the bourgeoisie whereupon the state may be expected to wither away and mankind live happily ever after.

I can imagine it all being very puzzling to future historians, assuming of course that there are any, and amuse myself by supposing, for instance, that somehow or other a lot of contemporary videos of television programmes with accompanying advertisements, news footage, copies of newspapers and magazines, stereo tapes of pop groups and other cacophonists, best-selling novels, films and other such material – all of this gets preserved like the Dead Sea scrolls in some remote salt cave. Then some centuries or maybe millenia later when our civilisation will have long since joined all the others that once were and now can only be patiently reconstructed out of the dusty ruins, incomprehensible hieroglyphics and other residuary relics. Archaeologists discover the cave and set about sorting out its contents, trying to deduce from them what we were like and how we lived. What would they make of us I wonder? Materially so rich and so powerful; aspiringly impoverished and fear-ridden. Having made such remarkable inroads into the secrets of nature, beginning to explore and perhaps to colonise the universe itself, developing the means to produce in more or less unlimited quantities everything we could possibly need or desire and transmit swifter than light every thought, smile or word that could possibly delight, entertain or instruct us. Disposing of treasure beyond calculation, opening up possibilities beyond conception yet haunted and obsessed by the fear that we are too numerous, that as soon as our numbers go on increasing there will be no room or food for us. On the one hand a neurotic passion to increase consumption, sustained by every sort of imbecile persuasion; on the other, ever increasing hunger and penury among the so-called backward or undeveloped peoples. Never, as our archaeologists will surely conclude, was any generation of men intent upon the pursuit of happiness and plenty more advantageously placed to attain their objective, who yet with amazing deliberation took the opposite course towards chaos not order, towards breakdown not stability, towards despair not hope, towards death, destruction and darkness; not life, creativity and light. An ascent that ran downhill;

plenty that turned into a waste land, a cornucopia whose abundance made hungry.

Searching about in their minds for some explanation of this pursuit of happiness that became a death wish, the archaeologists would be bound to hit upon the doctrine of progress, probably the most deleterious fancy ever to take possession of the human heart. The liberal mind's basic dogma, the notion that human beings as individuals must necessarily get better and better, is even now considered by most people to be untenable in the light of their indubitably outrageous behaviour towards one another. But the equivalent collective concept that their social circumstances and conduct must necessarily improve has come to seem almost axiomatic. On this basis all change represents progress and is therefore good. To change anything is *per se* to improve or reform it.

The archaeologists will also note how, with the abandonment of Christianity, the whole edifice of ethics, law, culture and human relationships based upon it, was likewise demolished; how sex and associated erotic and sterility rites provided the mysticism of the new religion of progress; an education, a moral equivalent of conversion, whereby the old Adam of ignorance and superstition and the blind acceptance of tradition was put aside and the new liberal man born: enlightened, erudite, cultivated. So the bustling campuses multiplied and expanded as did their facilities and buildings. More and more professors instructing more and more students in more and more subjects. As the astronauts soared into the vast eternity of space, on earth the garbage piled higher. As the groves of academe extended their domaine their alumni's arms reached lower. As the phallic cult bred so did impotence; in great wealth, great poverty; in health, sickness; in numbers, deception; gorging left hungry; sedated left restless; telling all, hiding all; in flesh united but forever separate. So we pressed on through the valley of abundance that leads to the wasteland of satiety, passing through the gardens of fantasy, seeking happiness ever more ardently and finding boundless despair ever more surely.

So the final conclusion would surely be that, whereas other civilisations have been brought down by attacks of barbarians from without, ours had the unique distinction of training its own destroyers at its own educational institutions and for providing them with facilities for propagating their destructive ideology far and wide, all at the public expense. Thus did western man decide to abolish himself, creating his own boredom out of his own affluence, his own vulnerability out of his own strength, his own impotence out of his own erotomania, himself blowing the trumpet that brought the walls of his own city tumbling down and, having convinced himself that he was too numerous, laboured with pill and scalpel and the syringe to make himself fewer, until at last, having educated himself into imbecility and polluted and drugged himself into stupefaction, he heeled over: a weary, battered, old Brontesaurus and became extinct.

I want just to conclude in this way. Christianity, I want to say, is indeed essentially a religion of hope. A new stupendous hope born of the Incarnation and creating a tidal wave of creativity and joy to revivify a world as tired, bored and decadent as ours. If now its impetus seems momentarily to be spent we need not despair. History, a continuing parable, whereby God's purposes are revealed for those with eyes to see, will continue to surprise. Who would ever have ventured to suppose that it would be from the Marxist East, not the ostensibly Christian West that would be heard the voice most clearly and eloquently stating once more the great propositions on which our Christian religion is founded, that through love not power, in humility not arrogance, we may best understand our creator's purposes for us here on earth. And that voice, Alexander Solzhenitsyn: one among many and speaking on behalf of many of his fellow countrymen, thereby demonstrating irrefutably that the whole stupendous effort made at such a fantastic cost in blood and tears to condition man to a purely terrestrial existence, the whole monstrous exercise in what is called in the jargon of Marxism "social engineering," has been a gigantic failure, a total fiasco, as such efforts must always be, including I might add crazed projects in our part of the world to sort out our genes in a somewhat more appropriate manner, to dispose of lives we consider worthless, to decide ourselves who should be born, and whom exterminated before leaving the womb. Even to achieve some sort of immortality by replacing our spare parts, liver, kidneys, heart, brain boxes, even as they wear out and so keeping us on the road indefinitely like vintage cars.

Should we not then rejoice that once more it has been revealed unmistakably that God never abandons us, that however sombre the darkness, his light still shines and however full the air may be of the drooling of Musak and the crackling of Newsak, truth will make itself heard. That in all conceivable and inconceivable human circumstance what the apostle Paul called "the glorious liberty of the children of God," the only enduring liberty there is, is always available to us. What then is this Christian hope, valid when first propounded and expounded some two thousand years ago, buoying up western man through all the vicissitudes and uncertainties of Christendom's twenty centuries and available today when it is more needed perhaps than ever before as it will be available tomorrow and forever whatever the circumstances whoever the individual or individuals in question and however inimical to it may be the shape of human society and the manner, the exercise and authority by those who rule over it.

The hope is simply that, by identifying ourselves with the Incarnate God, by absorbing ourselves in His teaching, by living out the drama of his life with Him including especially the Passion, that powerhouse of love and creativity, by living with and in Him we are suddenly caught up in the glory of God's love flooding the universe: every colour brighter, every meaning clearer, every shape more shapely, every note more musical, every true word written and spoken more explicit. Above all, every human face, all human companionship, each and every human encounter, of family affair, of brothers and sisters, with all the categories, beautiful or plain, clever or slow-witted, sophisticated or simple, utterly irrelevant. And any who might be hobbling along with limbs or minds awry, any who might be afflicted, particularly dear and cherished. The animals too, flying, prowling, burrowing and all their diverse cries and grunts and bellowings and the majestic hilltops and the gaunt rocks giving their blessed shade and the rivers making their way to the lakes and the sea. All, all irradiated with this same new glory. What other hope is there which could possibly compare with such a hope as this? What victory or defeat, what revolution or counter-revolution? What putting down of the mighty from their seats and exalting the humble and meek who then of course become mighty in their turn and fit to be put down? What going to the moon or exploration of the universe? A hope that transcends all human hoping and yet is open to all humans. Based on the absolutes of love rather on the relatives of justice; on the universality of brotherhood rather than the peculiarity of equality; on the perfect freedom which is service rather than the perfect service purporting to be freedom. It is precisely when every recourse this world offers has been explored and found wanting; when every possibility of help from earthly sources has been sought and is not forthcoming; when in the shivering cold the last faggot has been thrown on the fire and in the gathering darkness every glimpse of light has finally flickered out. It is then that Christ's hand reaches out, sure and firm; that his words bring their inexpressible comforts; that His light shines brightest, abolishing the darkness for ever, so that, finding in everything only deception and nothingness, the soul is constrained to have recourse to God himself and to rest content.

In that rich and somewhat vacuous country that I come from I have always wondered about the fellow who lives in bliss, acquiring ever more, newer and newer, goods and services. He is that 20th century species of homo sapiens known as the consumer. Leftists and rightists disdain him. Liberals and conservatives defer to him. And the upright Ralph Nader is forever springing to his defence against unscrupulous producers. As for me I wonder about his extravagance, his economic salubriousness, or his suffering at the hands of the cunning producers. I wonder about the smile on his face. Is his acquisitive existence as deeply satisfying as it so often appears? Some doubt that it is. I am not so sure. Obviously some consumers consume to forget, but I have observed vast numbers of exuberant consumers here and throughout the Western world who appear perpetually happy, wading through the years alotted them, tirelessly trying out all the newest marvels that the capitalist engine heaves up. Is the thing possible?

Malcolm Muggeridge is among the doubters. In fact everything created by the hand of man seems to attract Muggeridge's doubts. Whether in his long life he ever lived contentedly with the consumer's zeal for MORE – MORE consumer goods, MORE services, MORE pay, as a blunt and unphilosophical American labour leader once put it – I do not know. But he certainly indulged many of the century's materalist attitudes and ideologies. All of course left him rueful and unsatisfied. At the end of his binge he turned to faith in a hereafter, settling on the New Testament as his navigational chart.

The faith of Malcolm Muggeridge is, merci beaucoup, *a joyous one. Actually it is even elegantly sensuous, as is Chartres' rose window. Observe below in this famous interview where he speaks of worship being "a beautiful thing" and an "ancient ritual." That Muggeridge's joy has endured has surprised me, I having always suspected that the religious mind is a mind that drives out laughter. Muggeridge denies this, arguing instead that the religious mind understands the world's folly and guffaws; understands the world's ultimate promise and rejoices. Is he right, and can Muggeridge's spiritual journey be emulated?*

Here it is my turn to doubt. Just as I wonder about the existence of the blissful consumer, I wonder about the joyous faith of my friend. Is it really possible for the consumer to hum along through all the seasons of his life without a fugitive moment of metaphysical reflection and cosmic despair? Does he never need to soothe his spirit with abiding friendships, art, the pursuit of Aristotle's virtues, the faith of the twelve apostles? I am in awe of the powers of Muggeridge's faith, but I suspect that it opened to him because of the doubt that has always hounded him. What is to be the fate of those consumers who never know St Mugg's doubts? In all his singularly eloquent and affecting utterances both here and elsewhere he has never provided me with an answer. Nor has anyone else. What is to be the fate of the morally stupid?

R. Emmet Tyrrell, Jr.

Interview with William F. Buckley Jr.
For "Firing Line" 1978.

How Does One Find Faith?

MR. BUCKLEY: I propose on this occasion with Malcolm Muggeridge to do something a little unusual. We will devote the hour to exploring the phenomenon, if that is the right word for it, of religious faith. The conversation will be exploratory in nature and probably not adversary, and with very good reason it will focus much more heavily on the views and meditations of Malcolm Muggeridge than on my own. There is every reason for this decision, most prominently the superior wit, learning and experience of Mr. Muggeridge; but it is also true that in recent years he has emerged as perhaps the most eloquent English-speaking lay apostle of Christianity, and this he accomplished by encountering faith. When he turned against the devil, the devil was outnumbered.

In order to impose a little structure on the hour, I shall first be asking Mr. Muggeridge to give us an idea of how he came himself to God. After which, I propose that we examine the major sources of difficulty experienced by others who have not found faith, either because they reject it or because they are indifferent to it.

I suppose it is appropriate to add that we are taping this hour in the private workroom of Malcolm Muggeridge at his home deep in Sussex, sixty miles from London, where he and his wife have lived for the past twenty-five years, after as hectic a life abroad as that lived by any man of letters. He is currently at work on the third volume of his autobiography and co-operating in the production of an eight-hour series of television on his professional life.

To set out then, Mr. Muggeridge, tell us what it was that happened to you?

MR. MUGGERIDGE: This sounds a very simple question, but actually it's a very difficult question to answer. Of course, my evangelical friends are always rather disappointed that I can't produce a sort of Damascus road experience – you know, that I was such a person and then suddenly this happened, and I was such another person. But I can't. That isn't something that happened to me. This has been for me the unfolding of an enlightenment which is full of doubt as well as certainty. I rather believe in doubting. It's sometimes thought that it's the antithesis of faith, but I think it's connected with faith – something that actually St Augustine said – like, you know, reinforced concrete and you have those strips of metal in the concrete which make it stronger.

Mr. B: Well, is doubt the dialectical partner of faith?

Mr. M: I would say so.

Mr. B: That it forces continuous re-examination, which is why it is assumed that all the saints – or is it? – doubted.

Mr. M: If it's not assumed, it's certainly true that they did; and I would agree absolutely with that. The only people I've met in this world who never doubt are materalists and atheists.

Mr. B: But the doubts that they express are hardly theological.

Mr. M: I think that they have a sort of ludicrous

certainty that there is nothing transcendental to know, you see, but for me, at any rate, doubt has been an integral part of coming to have faith; nor has there been as I've said, any dramatic moment, any time when there it was, like has happened, for instance, to Pascal – people like that – or to Augustine. It's a process which I am quite sure will certainly continue until I depart from this life, which I shall fairly soon, and which maybe goes on into the next life for all I know, but an integral part of belief is to doubt. Now, why did this longing for faith assail me? Insofar as I can point to anything it is to do with this profession which both you and I followed of observing what's going on in the world and attempting to report and comment thereon, because that particular occupation gives one a very heightened sense of the sheer fantasy of human affairs – the sheer fantasy of power, and of the structures that men construct out of power – and therefore gives one an intense, overwhelming longing to be in contact with reality. And so you look for reality and you try this and you try that, and ultimately you arrive at the conclusion – great over-simplification – that really is a mystery. The heart of reality is a mystery.

Mr. B: Even if that were so, why should that mystery lead you to Christian belief?

Mr. M: Because it leads you to God. The mystery – and I think the best expression for it I've ever read is in a book I'm very fond of and I'm sure you know, called *The Cloud of Unknowing* and it's when you are aware of the cloud of unknowing that you begin to know, and what you know – to simplify and put it very simply, is God. That's the beginning of faith for me.

Mr. B: But that informal Christianity requires grace, but you seem to have described a purely deductive process.

Mr. M: The deductive process is the means, but faith is the motive force that takes you there.

Mr. B: In other words, if as an observer you cease to observe, then you don't have that motive force that grace contributes?

Mr. M: Absolutely right. That is the grace. It's exactly like falling in love. You see another human being and for some extraordinary reason you're in a state of joy and ecstasy over that person, but the driving force which enables you to express that and to bring it into your life is love. Without love, it's nothing; it passes. It's the same with seeking reality, and there the driving force we call faith. It's a very difficult thing to define, actually.

Mr. B: Well, why is it that scientists who devote themselves at least as avidly professionally as journalists to seeking out the truth, so many of them don't stumble on this mystery?

Mr. M: The greatest ones do, incidentally: Einstein, Whitehead, people like that. The very highest names in science do stumble on it and for precisely the same reason because the knowledge that they have through their researches is so limited, so fragile, and so inadequate that they, too, are forced to find some absolute.

Mr. B: Now, the use of the word "mystery" has been much disdained by sceptics as a too easy way to account for some of the hideous anomalous tortures of history: The Holocaust, to take something on a macrocosmic scale; the six-year old girl who dies of leukemia at another scale. Isn't it probably the case that such anomalies as these do more to encourage scepticism than anything in the divine order?

Mr. M: I don't think they encourage scepticism. On the contrary, I would say that they encourage credulity as a matter of fact. What they do is they present a dilemma to which reason provides no answer.

Mr. B: Yes.

Mr. M: And you can only find the answer through what is called mysticism, or indeed through what Blake called the Imagination, which is art.

Mr. B: Now, what did Blake mean by Imagination?

Mr. M: He meant putting it in one of my favourite sayings of his when he says – because it's so like this very medium we're working in now – he says, "They ever must believe a lie who see with not thro' the eye." He meant by Imagination seeing through the eye – seeing into this meaning of things rather than seeing things.

Mr. B: How would Blake have seen through to such a phenomenon as I mentioned – the death of a six-year old child?

Mr. M: Because he would see in it – there are some lines of his which I can't quote exactly from memory, but: "Joy and woe wove fine clothing for the soul divine." In other words, suffering, affliction, disappointment, failure – all these things – are an integral part of the drama of our human existence, and without them there'd be no drama. Let me tell you what will be a simple parable which I've often thought of. Some very humane, rather simple-minded old lady sees the play King Lear performed, and she is outraged that a poor old man should be humiliated, so made to suffer; and in the eternal shade she meets Shakespeare, and she says to him, "What a monstrous thing to make that poor old man go through all that," and Shakespeare says,

"Yes, I quite agree. It was very painful, and I could have arranged for him to take a sedative at the end of Act I, but then, ma'am, there would have been no play."

Mr. B: *Well –*

Mr. M: See my point?

Mr. B: *Yes, I see your point. On the other hand, I'm not sure that King Lear wouldn't have preferred that there should not have been a play than that he should have lived through Acts II and III.*

Mr. M: But then he would have been a cowardly man and, of course, he did in fact have to go through that suffering in order to understand why there had to be a play: and of course, in that marvellous speech of his – one of my favourite things in all Shakespeare – when he, to Cordelia says, "We two will go to prison," – you know – "and take upon's the mystery of things." It's a beautiful phrase, isn't it? It expresses exactly what I mean. This affliction has to be, and that is of course why one is drawn irresistibly as a Western European to the Christian faith and to Christ, because this is the central point: the cross. There's another parable I've often thought of. When St Paul starts off on his journeys, he consults with an eminent public relations man: "I've got this campaign and I want to promote the gospel." And the man would say, "Well, you've got to have some sort of symbol. You've got to have an image. You've got to have some sign of your faith." And then Paul would say, "Well, I have got one. I've got this cross." The public relations man laughed his head off: "You can't popularise a thing like that. It's absolutely mad!" But it wasn't mad. It worked for centuries and centuries, bringing out all the creativity in people, all the love and disinterestedness in people, this symbol of suffering; and I think that's the heart of the thing. Of course, it's what has been lost and why the faith is languishing; because it cannot take in that truth that we can learn nothing: and you know, as an old man, Bill, looking back on one's life, it's one of the things that strikes you most forcibly – that the only thing that's taught one anything is suffering, not success, not happiness, not anything like that. The only thing that really teaches one what life's about – the joy of understanding, the joy of coming in contact with what it really signifies – is suffering, is affliction.

Mr. B: *Well, you may recall the closing passages in* The Life of St Francis, *in which Chesterton remarks that whatever tortures he suffered as his life came to an end from whatever cause, one thing only one could know is that it was a happy man dying. Now the paradox – and I've witnessed it twice, people suffering agonies but who were spiritually serene – is: it may be easier for people who suffer through experience than for people who see them suffering.*

Mr. M: Certainly. I'm sure it is. I think because, first of all, there is an element you could almost call decency in us which says, "Well, I haven't had to suffer that myself and therefore it ill behoves me to point to it as a blessing."

Mr. B: *Yes.*

Mr. M: But of course, that would eliminate this idea of the cross, which was for everyone. Actually, in every time and in every age, this is demonstrated to us, and I think in our time it's been marvellously demonstrated by Solzhenitsyn and the other heroic people from the Soviet labour camps, all of whom say the same thing – the ones that have achieved spiritual perception through it – that there they learned this point, that it's through the affliction that you can see reality and that, therefore, as Solzhenitsyn himself says in his Gulag book, "Thank you, prison camp, for bringing this illumination into my life which otherwise I would have lost."

Mr. B: *Well, a reductionism of that point, however, you wouldn't applaud, namely that Stalin was God's prophet.*

Mr. M; No, but he might be God's instrument. In fact, he was, because in history it's impossible for anybody to function except as God's instrument because history is the scenario that God's written and the parts – all the parts – are necessary, just as the part of Judas was necessary for the Incarnation.

Mr. B: *If one indulges in that kind of predetermination, one strips that drama of spontaneity that, for instance, was shown by King Lear, doesn't one?*

Mr. M: But the thing is, it's not –

Mr. B: *How do you handle that paradox?*

Mr. M: It's freedom within the context of God's will, which is God's drama, and therefore anything that happens to us is in some degree God's will. We are participating in the unfolding of God's will. Supposing it's true, for instance, at this moment – which I think it probably is – that what we call Western Civilisation is guttering out to collapse. If you take that in purely human historical terms, this is an unmitigated catastrophe. You and I must beat our breasts and say that we lived to see the end of everything.

Mr. B: *But not quite the end of everything, because the gates of hell will not prevail against –*

Mr. M: Right, but also, historically speaking, what we love is coming to an end.

Mr. B: *Christendom.*

Mr. M: Christendom finished.

Mr. B: *It probably has finished.*

Mr. M: I think so. Why, certainly. But the point is, that is a catastrophe of God's purposes. I tell you, a thing I often think of as I beat my breast over what's going on in the world is St Augustine receiving the news in Carthage that Rome had been sacked. Well, I mean, that's an appalling thing. He was a very civilised Roman, and it was a dreadful thing that the barbarians should have come in there and have burned the place down.

Mr. B: *And he had been there for ten years.*

Mr. M: Absolutely. Now, what did he say to his flock? He said, "This is grievous news, but let us remember if it's happened, then God has willed it; that men build cities and men destroy cities, that there's also the City of God, and that's where we belong." To me, that's the perfect expression, and I think –

Mr. B: *Well, he said that's where we belong, but this is what we will never achieve.*

Mr. M: Right, but it's insofar as we're citizens of the City of God that we can be Christian in the City of Man.

Mr. B; *We can bear it.*

Mr. M: We can bear it.

Mr. B: *All right now, but this is in no sense a counsel of submissiveness, is it?*

Mr. M: Not at all. Not at all.

Mr. B; All right, how do you distinguish between the mandate that says acknowledge all adversity with a spirit of compliance and that counsel which says you are meant to struggle for your own livelihood, for your own principles, for your own country, for your own family?

Mr. M: Well, again you see, I think – and this is another great part of the realisation of reality in transcendental terms – that both those things are true, just as our Lord said to the people who were questioning him – cunningly, he said, "Yes, we owe things to Caesar, and we owe things to God." We are living in our time and it is our duty to acquit ourselves in the context of that time as truthfully, nobly, lovingly as we can.

Mr. B; Well, how does Caesar feature, for instance, in the struggle of the individual against physical adversity? You have, on previous occasions, spoken of the requirement – the ethical and religious requirement – that one struggle to live as long as one can. Your war against euthanasia is the extreme example of this. How does Caesar figure here in that struggle against submissiveness?

Mr. M: It simply means that you are not in a position – you're not competent – to decide that your own life should come to an end or that other lives should come to an end, that you must be engaged on the side of life and the sacredness of life in its earthly version – in its earthly terms – as you are a citizen of the earthly city. But, of course, your eyes are cast and, as you get to the end of your life more and more cast, in the direction of the City of God.

There are the two things, you see. I think one of the terrible difficulties we have in discussing these matters is this; that rooted in our minds is what Kierkegaard calls the either/or proposition. I mean, either we have free will or it is determination. This is not so. We have got free will, and not a sparrow can fall to the ground without God's will — or God willing it.

Mr. B: There's a complementarity somewhere?

Mr. M: Absolutely, and that is essential to know, and the scientific idea of either/or is a very disastrous proposition.

Mr. B: Now wait a minute. You're not denying the principle of contradiction, are you?

Mr. M: No.

Mr. B: You cannot be and not be at the same time.

Mr. M: But you can be, as the Incarnation showed — God can exist as a man and a man can be God. Why the terrific power of that drama, why it sheds such a light on the things we're talking about — that Christian drama — is precisely because it exemplified that. Jesus had to suffer. Otherwise, what's the cross? There's no sacrifice. At the same time, he had to be God because he was perfect.

Mr. B: "Christ without the crucifixion is liberalism," said Whittaker Chambers.

Mr. M: Yes, it's very good, that.

Mr. B: Well, these false disjunctions are probably the principle blocks, are they not, to a more universal acceptance of God?

Mr. M: They are, but we can't elucidate them in terms that the twentieth century wants.

Mr. B: *No, because the vocabulary is wanting, isn't it?*

Mr. M: Absolutely.

Mr. B: *It requires either a vocabulary so sophisticated as to be elusive except to the very few, or intuition, which is why the Russian illiterate kulak in Gulag understands, right?*

Mr. M: Yes, this is true, but at the same time, if you take the case of Pascal – it always interests me very much – who was the greatest mind of his time and leading scientist of his time, it was through his science and through his intellect that he arrived at the conclusion that the mind itself was sort of a cul-de-sac, and that he could only fulfil his life and grasp what it was about and relate himself to its true reality through faith. And that is the point. That's a marvellous definition of faith, you know, in the Epistle to the Hebrews, where it says, "Faith is the substance of things hoped for and the evidence of things not seen." In other words, it gives a shape to this marvellous hope that grows in us.

Mr. B: *Why wouldn't it also if it were illusory?*

Mr. M: If it were illusory? Well, I mean, yes, it could be so, but then we have to assume that with grace we can distinguish between illusory things and real things, that the mystery comprehends both.

Mr. B: *Your approach to God and to Christianity is through – to use a paradoxical term – the understanding of mystery, and yet –*

Mr. M: The acceptance of a mystery, Bill, is the way –

Mr. B: *Acceptance of the mystery.*

Mr. M: I don't understand it, because nobody ever will by its very nature.

Mr. B: That's why I said paradoxical.

Mr. M: Yes, but still, it is the acceptance of it. I bow my head in humility, I hope, and would wish to do and to say, "Thy will be done," meaning I accept totally the mystery of these circumstances.

Mr. B: How, then, do you handle – or do you bother – the Thomistic argument that the existence of God can be proved by a series of formal, logical propositions?

Mr. M: It has no interest to me.

Mr. B: No interest to you.

Mr. M: Not at all.

Mr. B: In other words, you wouldn't even bother to acquaint yourself with those propositions?

Mr. M: I might, as a mental exercise, amuse myself with it, but the one thing that I'm quite sure could never happen is that human reason could prove a transcendental truth. It can be compatible, as Newman showed again and again; it can be compatible with a transcendental truth.

Mr. B: There again, if you're using the word rigorously, "transcendental" is above reason.

Mr. M: Absolutely.

Mr. B: But on this programme a few months ago in an hour that was widely noticed, Mortimer Adler spoke his thesis, at the end of which he concluded that the existence of God was proven by ontological reasoning, and he did so by a very elaborate and active intellectual virtuosity which was rather arresting. However, he declined to go on so far as to say that it proved anything at all about the attributes of God. These, he said, were perhaps deducible by other means – revelation, for instance – so that he is prepared to say that the intelligent man must believe in God, but he need not expect to know what it is that is part of God's design. For instance, he need not affirm human immortality. This, is however, central to your belief, isn't it?

Mr. M: Again, you see – I have nothing but respect for Mortimer Adler, and I think that he should exercise his wits in the direction of God is much better than that he should exercise them in the direction of nuclear fission or something like that. That's all so, but at the same time, what appeals to me much more is the attitude of the founder of the Christian religion who said that, of course, it was children – it was simple people – who would understand what he was saying, and that when he was confronted with someone like Nicodemus, who was a sort of Adler –

Mr. B: He who seeth not and yet believes.

Mr. M: That appeals to me more, but I wouldn't for one moment detract from any effort that any human being should make in any capacity to reach out to this reality which is unattainable.

Mr. B: Well: you've studied and written about people who have searched after that reality, many of them using different modalities: Blake, Pascall, Bonhoeffer. . . .

Now let me ask you this, which is a question at the root of much current Christian concern: how far may a society go to defend itself against barbarians? In terms of formal instruction, the Catholics recall a statement made by Pope Pius XII – I think the year was 1948 – in which he said,

"Certain things are so valuable" – by which he meant, of course, divine institutions: the family, the church – "that they can rightly be fought for through the use of all one's resources." It was widely interpreted as baptising the use of nuclear fission for defence, and indeed during the past twenty to twenty-five years there seems to be a bifurcation: those Christians who say, "In no circumstances ought there to be a nuclear defence," and others who say, "Yes, because to treasure biological life so fiercely that one cares not at all about the circumstances within which it lived is the ultimate profanation – not Nagasaki." Have you thought your own way through to that conclusion in these terms?

Mr. M: I, like anybody else at this age, have thought much about it, and to me, I go back again to this saying of our Lord that we have duties to Caesar and duties to God. Our duties to Caesar require us, as for instance in 1939, to deal with a worldly situation that has arisen and risk our lives and –

Mr. B: Suppose one were to say, "I'm not willing to do it for Caesar. For Caesar I'm not willing to be the man in the bomber that presses the fateful button and eliminates the town of Leningrad but I am willing to do it for my family or for the survival of the Christian idea."

Mr. M: Bill, each man has to work this formula out for himself.

Mr. B: But have you worked it out?

Mr. M: Insofar as it's possible for me to do so, yes.

Mr. B: And you would understand yourself to be working for Caesar as you did when you fought in the second World War?

Mr. M: I would say there are circumstances in which I recognise my duty to Caesar. I admit to you that romantically – I've often longed for it – I would have loved to have been a monk, because if you're a monk, what you owe to Caesar is minimal – you have no family, you have no home, you have no possessions, all these things that involve us in Caesar's world. But we can't kid ourselves. If we have those things, we are involved. We have to weigh up the situation that arises and ask ourselves, "Does my duty to Caesar require me to do this?" In 1939 I had no doubt whatever that it did, and that duty to Caesar has to be fulfilled in all circumstances. It's quite useless to say that I can do my duty to Caesar with a crossbow, but I can't do my duty to Caesar with a nuclear bomb, because you're exerting power – force – in order to maintain an earthly position. But there is also duty to God; and the duty to God offers its own responsibilities; and we are left to decide for ourselves where those two duties lie: what we owe to Caesar; what we owe to God.

Mr. B: Well, "We are left to ourselves to decide," is a little atomistic, isn't it? Are you now anticipating a statement which you might make later that you recognise no teaching authority in Christianity?

Mr. M: I wouldn't say that I recognise no teaching authority at all. I think that particularly the historical Church with certain things that it has laid down – like its opposition to usury, its present opposition to birth control and so on – these things serve the greatest importance. But what I'm saying is this: that the Christian of modern times believes that a table of conduct can be derived, and you say, "This is the Christian programme. Vote for it. I'm in favour/I'm not in favour." There's no such thing. This life we have to live between the earthly city and the City of God, between time and eternity, between ourselves and our Creator; and we have to deal with the circumstances that arise in our individual life and in our collective lives on that basis.

Mr. B: Well, I think most people grant that: that, for instance, there isn't a Christian means of organising a society. There are Christian socialists, there are Christian individualists and so on. Where the duty of informed Christianity becomes relevant is primarily in the act of exclusion. Certain things you can't do, right? You can't kill people because you don't like the colour of their skin or their religious beliefs.

Mr. M: In certain circumstances, though, you are required to kill them.

Mr. B: Under certain circumstances you're required to kill them, but those circumstances are rather rigidly specified.

Mr. M: Even that requires a decision in the light of – for a Christian – in the light of his faith. I personally happen to believe that there are circumstances in which capital punishment is perfectly legitimate and desirable.

Mr. B: Well, join the Bible.

Mr. M: Yes. But that, again – I'm equally prepared to accept that a very devout Christian might reach a different conclusion.

Mr. B: Sure.

Mr. M: And I don't believe that there's a rule of thumb that you can say, "My dear fellow, you're not being a Christian because you believe in capital punishment," or that, "You're not being a Christian because you don't." In other words, we are required in our existence here to work this out, to relate ourselves – We're in the extraordinary position that our Lord was in as incarnate God. We are living in time. We belong to eternity.

Mr. B: So therefore the obligation of the Christian is simply to search out his conscience as rigorously as he can and make the decision that he deems appropriate.

Mr. M: That's right. It is to keep our eyes fixed – and that is what, as far as I know, all the mystics and saints have said, and many a theist says today, just as clearly. We have to find God, and keep our eyes fixed on Him.

Mr. B: Okay. Now, let me ask you this: there are few people more experienced than you in many fields – in literature and journalism and so on. What have you found to be the principle obstacle to a conscious search for spirituality? It seems to me that you see a world in which people reading books, seeing plays – whether current plays or plays written five hundred years ago – recognise the dimension of spirituality. They know that it's true. They know that it's extremely important. And yet they resist any search for it. They think it's unmodish, they think it's anachronised, and certainly they aren't willing to talk about it. It strikes me as odd in the same way that it would be odd if people knew about the existence of sex, but for some reason never exerted themselves in such a way as to stimulate that appetite.

Mr. M: Well, I see exactly what you're asking, and one can only speak of one's own personal life here. If there's one statement in the whole of the New Testament that rings true in the light of my own experience, it is that to be carnally minded is death, and to be spiritually minded is life and peace; and therefore, one of the agonies of living has been the eternal effort on the part of the collectivity in which I live –

Mr. B: *To mortify the flesh.*

Mr. M: (laughing) Yes. You see, that's one thing. Then, of course, even more basic is this ego which we have built into us and the overcoming of which is really the essence of life. I mean, it is to the degree to which you overcome it – the degree to which you eliminate this eternal dragging of every thought and inspiration you have to the core of your ego – that you could be said to live spiritually. So pride, carnality, egotism, cupidity – in fact, you know, it's a funny thing when you sit down to think this out, you arrive at, sort of, the case of our old friends, the seven deadly sins.

Mr. B: *Well, I know, but those are temptations. What I don't understand is this: I can imagine a swinging dinner party – by which I mean one at which the participants are intellectually curious, culturally diverse – in which you can bring up, let's say, an invention – some scientific discovery announced in that morning's paper having to do with splitting genes – or you can discuss the politics of Pakistan or you can discuss the latest play or the latest fashion or you can be curious about what it is that goes into the process of senility; you can talk about the pleasures that are taken from almost anything except the discovery of God. And I really, honestly don't understand, but I think you would agree it's true, that if you were in the middle of a dinner, to say, "I'd like to tell you about somebody who was dying from cancer and in the course of his racking torture, he picked up the Bible, and in the course of several days he discovered something that transported him into serene circumstances," I think conversation would stop, and people would think, "Oh God, St Mugg has spoken up again. Let's not invite him next time around."*

Mr. M: Well, let me answer this with the utmost candour that there have been times when, in such circumstances, I have felt that I ought to speak about God and I haven't. Right, but on the other hand, there have been circumstances I'm happy to say where I have and it's never failed to work. That's what's so extraordinary.

Mr. B: Yes, but usually – and I've observed you – usually when you do it, it's when you are addressing a thousand people or two hundred people or five thousand people and they have to submit to your oratorical architecture because they have no alternative, and you can then make it work. But although you can, as I say, do it in formal circumstances in informal circumstances you have not regularly done it.

Mr. M: Well I have. I have.

Mr. B: Well, you have because you have developed a certain audacity in this respect.

Mr. M: Yes, but I soon discovered that, far from being a kind of deflating social occasion such as you mentioned – sitting around a dinner table – the strange thing is that in ninety-nine cases out of a hundred it's an enormous stimulant.

Mr. B: I don't doubt your figure, because you've obviously experimented, but I have never experimented with it. I've been to a thousand social occasions at not one of which was the subject brought up.

Mr. M: But you could have brought it up.

Mr. B: No, I never could have brought it up because of the sense of the social situation.

Mr. M: What I would like to think is that one day you will, greatly daring; and I will make a bet with you here and now for a moderate sum of money that you will be surprised by the degree to which all these worldly people – as they seem to be worldly people or very much agnostic people and so on – how fascinated and attracted and interested they are by your proposition, and, of course, it depends in some degree how you put it out. I mean, the very simple Christian, probably an infinitely better Christian than I am, but who is a tremendously dogmatic person – we'll say Billy Graham, someone of that sort – this might be put in a way which would abash people. But I have discovered the opposite, that if you indicate in sincerity and truth that in the most wretched, inadequate way you have decided that there's absolutely no purpose in life except relating yourself to God and that on the Christian side there's only one way of doing that effectively and that is through the Incarnation, that the interest is quickened and that hostility which you expect to meet with, in fact, you don't.

Mr. B: Well, this may be the one point on which we are going to disagree, or else you move in much more sanctified company than I do. The term, a "Christer," is a pejorative term as socially used and in order to earn the reputation of being one, you have only to mention Christ, I would say, three times. Once per year might be permissible. Twice per year is tolerable. Three times per year is overdoing it. You become, a "Christer," and people think of you as not quite focused on the important things.

Mr. M: Well, I agree that of course people – the judgements that they might express – but I have never succeeded in expressing the heart of the Christian message with faith that it hasn't proved to be a stimulant rather than a depressant on conversation and has been responded to sympathetically rather than with hostility. But all the people sitting at that table, like yourself, have been mesmerised by this terrific consensus that Christ is outmoded; nobody is interested in Christ; he's a bore. But they've only been mesmerised, and you can break that mesmeric effect by simply refusing to accept it.

Mr. B: *At least you grant that this is social pioneering.*

Mr. M: Oh, it requires a certain effort, I quite agree, and I've often failed to do it. I've often joined in the rather shallow gossip that's going on.

Mr. B: *But I also have some of your speeches and very, very often they are highly allusive in their reference to – for instance, I remember a speech – you were called in several years ago to substitute for President Johnson or somebody to speak to the newspaper editors in Washington, and it happened that I addressed them the next day and they were still reeling from the impact of your performance, and so I rushed and read your speech – I think we published it, as a matter of fact and it was only in the very last sentence or two that the spinal column of the whole speech became evident when you made reference to "the most brilliant light that ever shone in this world, you continue to believe, shone in Bethlehem."*

Mr. M: Those tactics might be wrong, but they're not based on any lack of faith in what I'm trying to say.

Mr. B: *No, no, I'm not saying they are.*

Mr. M: No, no.

Mr. B: *They're procedural.*

Mr. M: Yes, it's procedural.

Mr. B: *Tactical.*

Mr. M: Tactical. And I think that certainly at a gathering of that kind I may have overdone it, you know, in –

Mr. B: Underdone it, you mean.

Mr. M: Well, overdone it in the sense of delaying the, as it were, the denouement – the unfolding of the denouement – but it would seem to me tactically necessary to lead up, rather, to it, than to plunge into it.

Mr. B: In speaking to the nation's newspaper editors, I suppose it would be a little bit like going to Plato's Retreat and talking about monogamy.

Mr. M: (laughing) It might be. Actually, there again, the response to that astonished me. Actually, it's been often my memory of dealing with American editors.

Mr. B: I've encouraged you.

Mr. M: Very much so, very much so.

Mr. B: All right, take the experience of Solzhenitsyn. The impact of Solzhenitsyn is so palpable that nobody can make him or it go away. It would be like attempting to live through Elizabethan England as though Shakespeare didn't exist. He is that much of a pressure. Now, having gone through what he's gone through, having probably had a more significant effect than anyone in this century in turning around political philosophical sentiment in Western Europe, there is a residue; and that residue is that he concluded that God is King, that Jesus Christ was the Incarnation. Now that terribly pains a great number of people who cannot deny the importance of Solzhenitsyn, but are horrified at the lengths to which he takes his own analysis, and they seek to pull the one Solzhenitsyn away from the other and they find that this is an impossible job.

Mr. M: Yes, it's very amusing to watch.

Mr. B: Yes, it is nonfissionable. Now, have you noticed that particular struggle?

Mr. M: Very much so. Very much so, and I tremble for him because I think that the pack is after him and because what he says is unbearable: that the answer to dictatorship is not liberalism, but Christianity. I mean, that is an unbearable proposition from their point of view, and it is where he stands. I've observed him, and I tremble a bit for his future because, as a foreigner living in an alien country, he's very much vulnerable. The rest of us can sort of lie low and keep quiet at times and so on. But still, it has been something wonderful to watch and, to more people than you might think, enormously heartening: that that is what this man should have to say instead of a lot of claptrap.

Mr. B: Sure, and the fact that he should go to Harvard and say exactly the same thing there he would say anywhere else. Do you remember on one occasion, you and I and Bernard Levin watched the famous interview by Solzhenitsyn that lasted about a half hour conducted by Mr Charlton – I think it was – of the BBC? And then we discussed it in the balance of an hour, and Bernard Levin, who began by saying, "Let me make myself plain. I consider Solzhenitsyn the most important living human being and the most ennobling; however, I wish to disassociate myself entirely from his theological conclusions." Now, is that disassociation increasingly hard, do you think?

Mr. M: Well, I think it's being increasingly exploited, you see, and when you can tear it in a hundred ways. They started off by never mentioning that he was a Christian. I mean, for a long time, he was made a hero of the cause of freedom, but it was never mentioned that an integral and essential part of it was his Christian belief. Now that he's so stressed that – quite sort of specifically stressed it – they attack from another direction, that we can't have this idea that only Christians can – why not Buddhists? – and all that sort of stuff.

Mr. B: Then they go on also to say that he's a theocrat which I don't think he is.

Mr. M: Not at all, not at all. Oh no, he's in some ways very similar. I found this last book of his – what is it called? *The Oak and the Calf* – I found that the best of all his books in a way because it describes him in very simple terms in the conclusions that he's reached and his relations with authorities in the USSR before he left.

Mr. B: Yes, it is his odyssey and an account of the pains required to save those invaluable literary properties.

Mr. M: Absolutely. Awfully touching for a writer, that he had the courage to go on writing, writing, without seemingly any possibility that he would be published.

Mr. B: Yes. Now, would you say that his presence has weighed heavily on the scale in respect of the search for God? Are many more people, as a result of Solzhenitsyn's writings, concerned about the theological alternative to secularism?

Mr. M: It would be awfully difficult to answer that, actually, because he's been, on the whole, interpreted very inadequately in the press and on the media, so that it's hard to say that; but I would think that perhaps more people than we think have been comforted. To me, as a person who was a journalist in the USSR in 1932, the idea that all these years later, one of the kind of favourite sons of the regime could emerge, speaking in these accents – and when I say, "favourite sons," I mean who emerges as an absolutely celebrated author for a time –

Mr. B: *Yes, well, he was sort of the intellectual complement of Svetlana. The notion that the only living child of Stalin should become a Western Christian, it must be terribly discouraging to the engines of Marxism.*

Mr. M: (laughing) The most extraordinary moment of my life, I got a two-page – two full-scale pages typed – fan letter from Svetlana, and I thought to myself, "If there's one thing that would have seemed to me utterly inconceivable in this world, it would be if Stalin's daughter were to write to me."

Mr. B: *(laughing) A fan letter from Stalin's daughter.*

Mr. M: And a very charming and perceptive letter.

Mr. B: *This was in reaction to one of your books?*

Mr. M: Well, it was in connection with Christianity, and particularly a book called *Jesus Rediscovered,* which she'd read. Life has such extraordinary surprises. It produces such amazing contradictions. That was certainly one of them. No, but I agree. I think that Solzhenitsyn – what he's done and his loyalty to his fellow prisoners in the Gulag and his tenacity with which he's gone on stating these deep truths about good and evil will seem in posterity one of the most amazing things of our time without any doubt. And don't forget – which people do forget – that Solzhenitsyn, after the coming out of *One Day in the Life of Ivan Denisovitch,* he could have just settled down to be the most famous writer in the USSR and just by keeping off a few delicate subjects could have had a life of Riley just like Maxim Gorki. And he wouldn't do it because he was determined to go on saying what he had to say.

It's a wonderful parable of our time.

Mr. B: Yes. Well, in the last couple of minutes, let me ask you this. You decline to generalise on the basis of your own approach to faith, the likely approach of other people. Is this because yours is idiosyncratic, or is it because you are convinced that it always comes individually?

Mr. M: Basically, I think it is the latter, that I'm absolutely sure that the ways to God are infinitely diverse, depending on temperaments and circumstances and hundreds of things; and one of the things that is, to me, off-putting in a certain amount of otherwise very creditable Christians – a manifestation in our time – is the idea there is a standard procedure that you're going to go that way, almost as though Bunyan had written in his pilgrimage that unless you actually took that path – you know, mark that on the map – you've had it. And I would, also in utter humility – because I don't in any way regard myself as in any way a good Christian or one who will approach the Pearly Gates other than in the most craven state of mind as to the record that will be in the hands of whoever keeps the gate –

Mr. B: Well, to say that you are an imperfect Christian is, for one thing, to acknowledge a congenital flaw in human nature, but to say that you approached God in a distinctive way is not to discourage, obviously, other people from seeking him out according to their own inclinations and temperament, right?

Mr. M: It's a terrible thing, you see, that as you get this idea of what being a good Christian is and you become stricken with your own inadequacy, your sense of yourself as a sinner – as a hopeless person – is magnified. I used to think it was an affectation in someone like St Francis or St Paul to say, "I am a prince of sinners," you know, but I see that – or Mother Teresa who was always the one to say, "I'm not worthy, I'm not worthy," – but it is to the extent that you can conceive this fulfilment, this spiritual fulfilment –

Mr. B: *It becomes true. Thank you very much, Malcolm Muggeridge.*

Interview with William F. Buckley Jr.
for "Firing Line" 1978.

Do We Need Religion?

MR. BUCKLEY: Recently from these quarters I spoke with Malcolm Muggeridge on the subject of the search for religion, his encounter with it, and the desolation of abomination that came from it. What we did not get into, and propose to do in this hour, is the question of denominationalism. Is he a member of a particular communion, and if not, why not? What is the role of the institutionalised church? Who and what are the enemies of the institutionalised churches? Why is it that the call to evangelism comes so embarrassingly, even to those whose belief in God is the central point of existence and claim on sanity? These questions, together with a few of the aphorisms collected by Mr. Muggeridge on the occasion of his seventy-fifth birthday, we explore in the study of Malcolm Muggeridge, author of over twenty books, a journalist with few, if any, peers, who, in his retirement, is working on a third volume of his autobiography. This he is doing while the BBC puts together an eight hour special on his professional life. He says he has visited America for the last time, and if this is indeed the case, we can be grateful, as we seldom have been before, for the benefits of television.

I'll begin, then, by asking what I suppose is the most obvious question, particularly inasmuch as I am one myself: why are you not a Catholic?

MR. MUGGERIDGE: It's not altogether easy to answer that

actually, Bill. I've, believe it or not, longed to be a Catholic. It's something that I've longed for as though it were the most marvellous thing, but I've never been able to feel in honesty that I could present myself for instruction, and it's extremely difficult to know why. The truth is, I think, that I take a very pessimistic view of the Catholic Church, despite the very brilliant Pope you've now got. It seems to me that it's dropping to pieces; and of course it had a severe blow after the Vatican Councils. Therefore, I would be joining something of which I was enormously critical, and this isn't really an honourable thing to do.

Mr. B: That's never bothered you before.

Mr. M: I've never contemplated anything so serious as joining a church. I mean, even if you were to turn to mundane things – joining a club – if you were to join it quite confident that you were going to challenge all its rules and have rows with all its members, it would be rather a foolish step to take.

Mr. B: You once called yourself an imperfect Christian. Is this a sign of pride?

Mr. M: I don't think so, because I would have no troubles if I felt that I could go as a sinner into the Church. I'm sure many people have. It's a feeling that I would go there in some degree under false pretences. I don't know. There was an incident which, trivial in itself, played quite a part in my decision not to become a Catholic. The time when I was nearest to going and asking to be instructed – and I'd planned that I would go to Father D'Arcy because I had a great love for him – it was when I was rector at Edinburgh University, and I ran into a row there which you might have heard of when I was asked, as rector, by the students –

Mr. B: To supply contraceptives.

Mr. M: That's right – to recommend that they should be given, unquestioningly, free supplies of contraceptives by the University medical unit, and I refused to do this and there was a hullabaloo. And I thought to myself, you see, "Well, there are a thousand Catholics in the University, and they'll be on my side anyway. I've got a thousand men on my side." What happened was that the first big blast against me was a letter in *The Scotsman* by the Roman Catholic chaplain at the University saying what a monstrous thing this was that I had done.

Mr. B: Excuse me, but why was it monstrous?

Mr. M: It was monstrous, according to him, because it accused the students of wanting to be promiscuous; but in a letter I wrote in answer to it, I said I wondered what the Reverend Father thought they wanted the contraceptives for? Was it to save up for their wedding day? He offered no answer to that. But then I thought that somebody would give him a very big reprimand. But no such thing happened. Then I thought he'd almost certainly become a bishop. But that didn't happen either. What has happened is the perfect payoff of the whole episode: he's now rector of Edinburgh University (laughter).

Mr. B: And did they get their contraceptives?

Mr. M: Oh yes, oh yes. But there was nobody who reprimanded him. One Jesuit monk wrote to me and said that he thought it was monstrous and that he'd written to this Father and suggested that he should apologise to me, but nothing came of that. Anyway, it was a small episode, but it gave me the feeling that – one of the things I admired the Church for so much was *Humanae Vitae.* I think it's absolutely right that when a society doesn't want children, when it is prepared to accept eroticism unrelated in any way to its purpose, then it's on the downward path. So I admired it so much, and then I realised that since I was involved in this row, their adherence to it was very, very ceremonial rather than actual. They didn't really believe in it themselves, and I don't – I mean, I think the figures of population and so on in some places like Quebec show that they don't believe it, and they haven't practised it.

Mr. B: Well, I'm, to put it lightly, stupified that you would make a decision whether or not to extend your loyalty to an institution based on the behaviour of some of its communicants. I can't imagine any time in history when anybody would have become a Catholic if he had been so easily put off.

Mr. M: That's true. That obviously wasn't a major thing, Bill, but what it did was kind of crystallised certain feelings I had that these things that I so enormously admired – and of course the same thing is true of the Mass. The happiest time I ever had in terms of worship was when Kitty and I were staying in a village behind Nice and there was an old-fashioned priest there and we went to Mass in the church there every morning, and I absolutely loved it and I never felt more sort of happy spiritually. But –

Mr. B: You're not saying that the Church isn't clubbable?

Mr. M: No, not at all, but that the things in it that hold my admiration are the very things that it's turning its back on – that I would be involved in endless controversies connected with them.

Mr. B: Well, you would be the millionth Catholic who was.

Mr. M: (laughing) Yes, I suppose so. But can't you see that perhaps it's an excuse I've invented myself. It's quite possible.

Mr. B: *You have no problems, then, I take it, with the Apostles' Creed?*

Mr. M: None at all.

Mr. B: *Or with apostolicity?*

Mr. M: Not at all. I assent to it. Or the infallibility of the Pope; that doesn't worry me at all. I can see the purpose of all those things, and I see the context of people that I so admire – like St Augustine and St Francis – who were ready to accept all that; and the idea that I would come forth and say, "No, I couldn't possibly be in a church when the Pope claims to be infallible –"

Mr. B: *Well, of course, that was some time after –*

Mr. M: It was after, of course, but things of that sort, you see? None of that has ever presented any difficulty. On the contrary, it's the feeling that the Church itself is moving from these basic beliefs that is distressing. Or maybe it's just some kind of instinct.

Mr. B: *But there can't have been a more resonant reaffirmation of them than by the present Pope. I'm not here to try to convert you. I'm just exploring.*

Mr. M: No, no, no. I know. This is absolutely true, and of course, it has given great joy to many people because of that, but it still remains the case that I can't join it; and I'll have to meet my Maker not having joined it. Probably I'll get a frightful pasting in purgatory for it, but I can't help it. No.

Mr. B: *Now, what about the intra-Christian community quarrels? What importance do you attach to them?*

Mr. M: Well, I think there's only one quarrel in the institution of churches that seems to me to be serious and vital – and of course, the Roman Catholic Church is not equally, but also involved in it – and that is the quarrel between those who accept our Lord saying that his kingdom is not of this world and those who believe that they can construct a kingdom of heaven on earth. That is the basic quarrel.

Mr. B: Utopians, yes.

Mr. M: Yes, Utopians. And I, you know, with all the feeling I have in the world, I am against the Utopians and on the side of the –

Mr. B: And you see the Utopians as figuring primarily in which sect?

Mr. M: Well, I think that they figure more in the Protestant sects, especially perhaps the poor old Church of England which I technically belong to, but which is an appalling – probably the most awful shambles that's ever existed, even in the history of institutional Christianity. But it's becoming very noticeable in the Catholic Church in certain sects and particularly, for instance, in Latin America I would have said, without knowing a great deal about it. Anyway, that is the big row, and, of course, the body that I once described as the *pons asinorum* of all Christian endeavours – the World Council of Churches – is a kind of classic example of it which I think does immense and unbelievable harm to the Christian faith. And I greatly respect the Catholic Church for keeping out of it, even though it sends an observer there.

Mr. B: Is your quarrel with the World Council of Churches based on its accent on secularism and secularist achievements?

Mr. M: Yes, and plus its devastating attacks on places like South Africa and total acquiescence in places like the USSR, which is represented there by clergy from the stooge Russian Orthodox Church.

Mr. B: What role has the community – the flock – to play in intensifying the Christian experience? It is by various denominations thought of as a shared experience – right? – a joint experience. You are not only your brother's keeper, but you are in a sense your brother's companion. The notion of congregation is theological in its derivation, I think.

Mr. M: Yes.

Mr. B: Do you have a special attitude towards people who say, "I don't need a church. I don't need other communicants. I'll just go out in the fields and communicate with my Maker?"

Mr. M: (laughing) I don't particularly like that, but I can't very well criticise it because I could be said to be in it myself. Why I don't think I'm really in it is because there's nothing I long for more.

Mr. B: Well, let me ask you this question: would you, in the spirit of Immanuel Kant, universalise your own experiences? That is to say, "For the reasons that I do not join, I counsel others not to?"

Mr. M: No, I wouldn't dream of doing that. I mean, as a matter of fact, it happens sometimes people who are about to become Roman Catholic for some reason come and see me, and I always give it my blessing. I think it's marvellous. It just is something I can't do myself. There's one other thing in it I haven't mentioned that it is not very important, but it's worth mentioning. Now, of course, I'm thought of as a person who is an aspiring Christian or a Christian or at any rate whose heart is in the Christian position. And as, through television, a number of people recognise my aged mug, it quite often happens that people come up to me as fellow Christians might come up and sort of just shake your hand and you go to a restaurant and – it once happened to me, a waiter comes padding along behind you and you think, "I haven't given a big enough tip," and he wants to say, "I'm a Christian too."

Mr. B: So in that sense you are already a member of a community, even though it's not a formal communion.

Mr. M: Right, and also I've a feeling, first of all, that I would never want to ask these people, "Which denomination do you belong to?" And therefore, in a way, to identify oneself, even with something so marvellous as the Catholic Church, would be in a sort of way letting some of those people down.

Mr. B: I understand what you mean. To belong to any organisation is in a sense an act of exclusion.

Mr. M: It is.

Mr. B: And it is once again a paradox that that which is considered to be incorporative of society should also be, in a sense, exclusivist.

Mr. M: Absolutely.

Mr. B: After all, the rites, which I take it you will never submit to, require you to abjure a whole series of things that are read out, and you say, "I do abjure them, I do abjure them" – all the famous heresies and so on. Well, having – I won't quite say disposed of that question –

Mr. M: Yes, it's too big.

Mr. B: Let me try out on you, because I think I see a line that connects them, a series of rather provocative answers that you gave to The New York Times *when, on the occasion of your seventy-fifth birthday, they asked you to formulate some of the conclusions you've arrived at.*

Mr. M: I remember well.

Mr. B: Okay. No.1 – this is you speaking – "When mortal men try to live without God, they infallibly succumb to megalomania or erotomania or both: the raised fist or the raised phallus, Nietzsche or D.H. Lawrence. Pascal said this and the contemporary world abundantly bears it out." Isn't that a bit exaggerated?

Mr. M: I don't think it is, actually, because – I see why you say it's exaggerated, but I –

Mr. B: It's because you say, "infallibly". That's the operative affront.

Mr. M: Yes, well, certainly Western society bears it out, doesn't it? It is megalomania, the absolute insistence that the only thing that matters is the ego, the individual person . . . .

Mr. B: Well, the theologian Robert Fitch wrote a wonderful book ten or fifteen years ago called The Odyssey of the Self-Centred Self, *in which he says that – we now call it the "me" decade – that man, who used to be concerned with God, is now concerned with himself, but there were these intermediate phases: he was concerned with nature at one point; he was concerned with science at one point. And he sees this evolution as having come to megalomania. But is it not possible that you would be concerned with something other than God or yourself?*

Mr. M: Well, of course, you have many other preoccupations, but I would contend that those occupations themselves run into the sand unless they are related to God, the ultimate reality; that we can't find anything even to occupy our time effectively if we leave God out; and that it simply is true that man cannot exist in the universe, in time, on his own steam. It doesn't make any sense. It can't be.

Mr. B: All right. Now let me ask you this: when you use the word "erotomania", do you use it literally, or are you using it as a comprehensive term for sensuality in general, which would include, for instance, eating and drinking?

Mr. M: I suppose you could take it as both really. I must say that I think that as our society is increasingly preoccupied with one single appetite – namely the sexual appetite – that I perhaps did mean erotomania mainly, but it should equally take in the others, which are part of the same thing. Perhaps the better word should have been "carnality".

Mr. B: Carnality, yes.

Mr. M: Would have been a better word. But of course, we see it in this preoccupation with sex, and I must now say this: that recently, I've had occasion to read through a lot of old diaries that I'd forgotten, and reading through them has been particularly disagreeable because it shows how preoccupied I was myself with Eros – how much of my time and hope and pleasure seemed to be connected with that. And I look back on it as a kind of servitude, really. And I'm sure it's true when the history of the twentieth century is written it will be seen, as was true of course of the last stages of the Roman Empire – this utter preoccupation with, not reproduction, but with the mere excitements accompanying reproduction.

Mr. B: In what category would you put the satisfaction of aesthetic appetites?

Mr. M: Obviously, a very high level of this. Indeed, the aesthetic appetite is moving into the field of mysticism, which is precisely where we meet God, so that I would include — as we said in our previous talk — Blake's concept of the Imagination as part of man's mystical life.

Mr. B: Let me skip then to your Proposition No.4, because it's related to what you've just finished saying: "A God who chose to generate genius capable of producing a Missa Solemnis *or a Chartres Cathedral would surely be unwilling to confine his creativity to so banal and mechanistic a procedure as natural selection. It would be as though* King Lear *had come off a conveyor belt or* Paradise Lost *out of a computer." Are you saying quite directly that God was the animating genius behind great art?*

Mr. M: Most certainly.

Mr. B: What about great art that is totally secularist in its conception?

Mr. M: I don't think it's great. I know this is a dogmatic statement, but I don't think it is. I don't think there's any great art which does not have in it some sort of transcendental significance.

Mr. B: What would you say about The Tempest?

Mr. M: I would put *The Tempest* in the whole realm of Shakespeare, and I would say that in Shakespeare there is an enormous contribution towards this awareness of man's destiny which is an expression of transcendentalism.

Mr. B: Have you a thesis as to why Shakespeare never accosted the point directly?

Mr. M: Yes. I think he was treading on a hot plate in the Elizabethan Age, and although he ridiculed the Puritans and things like that, I think that to embark upon any kind of theological basis would be something that, first of all, would not have appealed to him personally, but equally, would have had great dangers. People were being bumped off, weren't they, at that time?

Mr. B: Yes. Well, he lived in pre-Cromwellian times, but religious controversies were heated. But can you explain the singular absence of religious metaphor in Shakespeare?

Mr. M: I wouldn't say religious metaphor. I would say there was an absence possibly of Christian metaphor, but not of religious metaphor. In fact, it's absolutely bristling with it, particularly the great tragedies.

Mr. B: I should have said Christian metaphor.

Mr. M: Yes, I think there is an absence of that, and again it was a troubled time, wasn't it? The metaphysical poets were coming along, but that was a different age.

Mr. B: Well, what you've just said in fact relates to another of your opinions. Shakespeare died in 1616, which is approximately halfway through a period of thirty or forty years when, it can roughly be said I suppose, that the knowledge of the physical universe doubled, trebled, quadrupled, ending with the Principia. *It was an age in which human beings were urged to cultivate knowledge. Along you come four hundred years later with the following put-down: "Accumulating knowledge is a form of avarice and lends itself to another version of the Midas story, this time of a man so avid for knowledge that everything he touches turns to facts; his faith becomes theology; his love becomes lechery; his wisdom becomes science; pursuing meaning, he ignores truth."*

Mr. M: Well, I stand by that.

Mr. B: Okay, let's examine that. You're saying that the exploration of knowledge leads to kind of an arid accumulation of it.

Mr. M: Yes, and to feeling that knowledge has value in itself, apart from its relation to truth, which is something quite different. Incidentally, again talking of Blake, you know what he wrote across his copy of Bacon's *Advancement of Learning* – which was, of course, a very important book in history. He wrote, "Good news for Satan's kingdom." Now, I think, he's absolutely right. It doesn't mean that men mustn't seek knowledge, but they seek knowledge in order to understand truth better. But there's no knowledge itself apart from truth, and it's a different thing from truth. It's not just worthless, but harmful. And it's very much the case now. It's what our universities are largely doing, and therefore they're producing people –

Mr. B: Nihilism.

Mr. M: Yes, absolutely.

Mr. B: Well, a search for knowledge is not – or is it? – an invitation to invincible ignorance if the search becomes more important than the discovery?

Mr. M: Yes, I think it can be that, and there are many people – I'll name no names – among the more famous dons of the age who illustrate that to perfection. Again, you have, of course, in Pascal the opposite trend, in which he, who had acquired so much knowledge, saw it as absolutely worthless in itself. What we are concerned with is truth; and knowledge can be part of truth, but it is not truth.

Mr. B: In what dismissive way did you use the word, "theology," when you said, "His faith becomes theology?"

Mr. M: Well, it becomes stating certain dogmatic propositions which, though they may play a part in building up a concept of faith, detached from faith are quite worthless.

Mr. B: You are using the word as one might use "scientific", as distinguished from "scientific".

Mr. M: Precisely, precisely, precisely. But I'm not against knowledge, you know. I mean, I think every single thing that men do can be done because God has equipped them to do it and, therefore, in doing it, they can be serving God's purposes; but they can also use it in such a way that it negates God's purposes.

Mr. B: Mightn't it be said with some confidence that the search for historical and sociological knowledge teaches us what in fact you have formulated in one of your propositions? The way you put it is as follows: "There can never be good governments that are less bad than others. The quest for a perfect government ends infallibly in anarchy or the Gulag Archipelago." Now, that is an anti-Utopian conviction of yours that I happen to share, and it once again, using the Christian metaphor, distinguishes the City of Man from the City of God, does it not? But isn't it true that a pursuit of knowledge teaches us the limitations of government?

Mr. M: It should, but it doesn't always. In that it's done

for itself alone, it tends to increase people's arrogance rather than teach them humility, which is of course the condition of all awareness of truth. Simon advises that the only purpose of seeking knowledge through education is to made men realise the inadequacy of their knowledge and, in realising that, of course, then they are brought nearer to God. But when you make knowledge an end in itself, then it's destructive of truth.

Mr. B: Let's examine this in concrete terms. Suppose you were to encounter someone who, at age thirty, determined to consecrate the whole of his life and all of his energies to the search for the causes of cancer. Are you implying that the consecration is going to strip him of his capacity to put cancer in proper focus?

Mr. M: No, because I think that he would be actuated by love, by humane feelings, by a desire to deliver –

Mr. B: It might be vanity.

Mr. M: It might be vanity, but if he were to be effective at it, you would find that vanity wouldn't get him very far actually. It's the quest for something that will deliver mankind from one of their scourges that makes such a quest near to God; otherwise, if it were purely vanity – and I think you see that in the developments of things like heart transplants where the vanity of surgeons to show that they can do these things is evident.

Mr. B: It becomes exhibitionism.

Mr. M: Yes, and it is very noticeable. That's only an extreme example. But you could go further and say that the dreadful dilemmas which doctors have created for themselves through the development of their knowledge is due to the fact that that knowledge has been sought for self alone, and it has been sought for self alone by regarding human beings as mere carcasses, bodies, leaving out the dimension of the soul. That's the explanation of the dreadful plight into which they've got through the very brilliance of their discoveries. It's an amazing parable for us to watch and meditate upon.

Mr. B: The injunction to seek out perfection while recognising that you can never achieve it, to seek the company of the saints – the standard term is "the counsel of perfection" – encourages absorption with the end in mind. I cited the case of the man who wants to find the causes of cancer. Let us change the example to the man who seeks to make the most beautiful music. Toscanini was an intolerable human being and a great genius as a conductor. We are all used to reading about how difficult it is to get along with genius. There are, of course, fabulous exceptions. Bach was a cozy family man, but for every one like him there is the Napoleon or the Alexander or whoever. Now, in attempting a Christian understanding here, what is it that goes slightly wrong? Looking for something for the sake of gratifying yourself rather than of serving something?

Mr. M: The ego.

Mr. B: The ego.

Mr. M: Same old ego, you see. One thing to be this famous conductor on whom all eyes are cast, not in utter humility – and I go back to the word humility, which is the key word, which is wanting to produce in the best possible way this marvellous music which would carry men away from their egos, away from their mundane existence, into the spiritual world. That's the point, so that we always come back to it: that it is what they are doing it for that matters. Of course the Christian says that essentially we do it for the glory of God. I think of the people building

Chartres Cathedral, say, and doing it for the glory of God. We don't even know who they were.

Mr. B: *No, but we certainly know they made enormous sacrifices because there was a kind of residue –*

Mr. M: Yes.

Mr. B: *– in the twelfth century –*

Mr. M: But a man who builds a great skyscraper so that everybody says, "That's his skyscraper. He built that." That's the opposite thing. And in that the twentieth century has produced interested endeavour, it has spread ugliness through the world, because egotism is very ugly. Man thinking of himself as one of the great marvels of creation is an ugly thing. Man thinking of himself as one single, tiny figure in the whole creation of God – one member of this enormous family that God has created – that's when he's near to truth.

Mr. B: *No, but man is entitled to think of himself as not only all-important in the sense of his supreme mission of pleasing God and achieving immortality, but also as the paradigm by which he understands the injunction to love others as oneself. Is that not correct? If one despised oneself and one's love of others were equal to that of oneself –*

Mr. M: You would have to despise others.

Mr. B: *– it would be insufficient.*

Mr. M: That wouldn't be right at all.

Mr. B: *No.*

Mr. M: But if you are aware of yourself as a fallen creature, which you are told to be –

Mr. B: Then you love others in the knowledge of their imperfection.

Mr. M: That's right.

Mr. B: Okay. Now, one of the things that Christianity suffers from is its association with asperity and desiccation. Mencken's redolent put-down that, "A Puritan is somebody who is afraid that somebody somewhere is happy," influenced the attitudes of an entire age. The pleasure of Christianity can be very intense, you have specified, and in one of your propositions to the New York Times, *you wrote: "Mystical ecstasy and laughter are the two great delights of living, and saints and clowns their purveyors, the only two categories of human beings who can be relied on to tell the truth; hence, steeples and gargoyles side by side on the great cathedrals." Now, are they telling the same truth or are they giving you a dialectic form from which truth emerges?*

Mr. M: Well, I think a bit of both, but let's think of the steeple and the gargoyle. The steeple is this beautiful thing reaching up into the sky admitting, as it were, its own inadequacy – attempting something utterly impossible – to climb up to heaven through a steeple. The gargoyle is this little man grinning and laughing at the absurd behaviour of men on earth, and these two things both built into this building to the glory of God.

Mr. B: Now, he's not laughing at evil, is he?

Mr. M: No.

Mr. B: He's laughing at pomposity.

Mr. M: He's laughing at the inadequacy of man, the pretensions of man, the absolute preposterous gap – disparity – between his aspirations and his performance, which is the eternal comedy of human life. It will be so till the end of time, you see.

Mr. B: And what is it that is the principle source of laughter? The difference between human nature and human performance.

Mr. M: The difference between human nature and human performance.

Mr. B: Human aspiration is not laughable, is it?

Mr. M: Well, it is, because it's –

Mr. B: Only when it's excessive. Why.

Mr. M: Because of always aspiring to do more than they can actually do. That's why –

Mr. B: But to aspire to do good is not to aspire to do too much.

Mr. M: No, but –

Mr. B: Mother Teresa aspires to do good and does.

Mr. M: Well, actually she doesn't aspire to do good. She's the first person to say that what she does is simply to love her neighbour as herself. I mean, the idea of aspiring wouldn't really occur to her. When people aspire – and I've used it of myself in this talk, actually, as an aspiring Christian, and it's slightly fraudulent in this context really, because it means that you're hoping to be a marvellous Christian –

Mr. B: *Well, if you aspire to please God, you're not necessarily ridiculous, are you?*

Mr. M: You're on the path. You're on the path. You're on the right path.

Mr. B: *One of my favourite short stories is the one of "Our Lady's Juggler." You recall that? Anatole France's.*

Mr. M: I don't remember it, at any rate.

Mr. B: *Well, you have a recently arrived monk at a monastery of very learned men, and on the feast day of Mary, each of them performs that at which he is a virtuoso. There is the organist, there is the composer, there is the poet. And this poor little man, what he was before he entered the monastery was a juggler, a common juggler who went around the little towns of France and a few people threw a few pennies at him and he lived that way. So when the turn came for him to perform, he passed on the grounds that he had no qualification to serve. But then, at ten o'clock that night, when all of his companions had gone to sleep, he tiptoes into the chapel with his old balls –*

Mr. M: Does his act.

Mr. B: *– and he does his act.*

Mr. M: I like that.

Mr. B: *And at that moment, the statue of Our Lady comes to life and she smiles.*

Mr. M: I like that.

Mr. B: *It's an exquisite story, and it's the nearest thing to egalitarianism that I can think of in much of Christian literature. But here is somebody who aspires to please about whom you can hardly say that what he did was laughable.*

Mr. M: No, no. It's beautiful. It was also a bit funny, but rightly so.

Mr. B: Objectively, it was funny.

Mr. M: Yes, and that funniness is a beautiful thing in it.

Mr. B: Yes.

Mr. M: Which I'm sure he would have rejoiced over also. But what I think – perhaps this aspiring business, I carried it too far, but aspiring means that one – I love this idea of humility – of the recognition that with the best will in the world and the most ardent love of God, we still are utterly, hopelessly inadequate in our performance. When we try to write about eternity and we try to write about truth, what we're doing is simply the scribble of children before they've learned their alphabets.

Mr. B: But that simply isn't true. The people who built Chartres did not do anything except create something very beautiful.

Mr. M: Yes, but when they look at Chartres in eternity, it seems like a piffling little monument compared with what it's celebrating.

Mr. B: Well, it can only be that if you assume an imagination great enough to think of it as trifling, but it is very hard to imagine a context in which Bach's B Minor Mass *is trifling.*

Mr. M: I think Bach, now, in eternity you would find that he would eagerly agree with me that it's the most ridiculously inadequate piece of music ever written. I mean, that's what is marvellous.

Mr. B: I think you certainly strain credulity, because on the one hand, you begin by saying only God could have created something so beautiful, and then you say this trifling –

Mr. M: It's because when a man is actually with God, then he sees that what he's tried to do, and in our terms done so marvellously, amounts to something which is utterly inadequate. That's what I'm saying: that what the steeple is reaching up to is so far, far away, that the steeple, beautiful as it is – let's say one of the English – Salisbury Cathedral is a beautiful steeple, but what is it compared with the sky into which it is reaching? And it's in the realisation of that comparison that this awareness of, on the one hand, the absurdity of our efforts, and on the other, the inadequacy of them.

Mr. B: In pursuit then of tolerable pleasure – from which we have excluded vanity, erotomania, gluttony – you touch on happiness, and you write: "Another disastrous concept is the pursuit of happiness, a last-minute improvisation in the American Declaration of Independence substituting for the defence of property. Happiness pursued cannot be caught, and if it could, it would not be happiness."

Mr. M: Well, that's true.

Mr. B: Well, there are a lot of paradoxes there.

Mr. M: But it's true.

Mr. B: It's true if you say that the pursuit of happiness has to be asymptotic – you can never quite get there. You can get closer and closer and closer, but you never quite get there. However, the pursuit of happiness is supposed to bring happiness.

Mr. M: But it's a wrong approach.

Mr. B: It's the pursuit that brings the happiness, not the acquisition of it, isn't it?

Mr. M: I think the pursuit is a misguided concept because I think the thing about happiness is that it happens – it comes to us. It comes to us mysteriously. Again, when our relations with God are harmonious –

Mr. B: But spiritual exercises are a form of pursuit, aren't they? Prayer.

Mr. M: Prayer is not really a form of pursuit. The purpose of prayer – of all spiritual exercises – is to get nearer to God. To be near to God is to be happy, and suddenly happiness floods your being; but if you were to pursue that, say, "I must get near to God in order to be happy," you wouldn't get near to him and you wouldn't be happy. That's what I'm trying to say.

Mr. B: It has to be providential.

Mr. M: Unchased.

Mr. B: It has to be providential.

Mr. M: Yes. It has to come about as part of a state of mind, and a state of mind which, in my opinion, insofar as it can be defined at all, is based on this relationship with God, this readiness, this preparedness to say, "Thy will be done." It's an incredible thing the joy that comes of being able to say and mean that.

Mr. B: *When you say, "Thy will be done," what you are really contracting to do is to accept that which happens, right?*

Mr. M: Yes, to say that it is your –

Mr. B: *And therefore you are disciplining yourself –*

Mr. M: Right.

Mr. B: *– to a kind of abjection which is in harmony with what Providence ordains.*

Mr. M: And then suddenly you're happy.

Mr. B: *And suddenly you're happy.*

Mr. M: You're happy. You're not happy when you say, "There is happiness. I must go after it." And of course, unfortunately, what it's amounted to – and had to amount to – particularly in our world today is the pursuit of pleasure, which of all the things that men go in for is the most fatuous and the most, ultimately, agonising.

Mr. B: *Was Sisyphus happy?*

Mr. M: Sisyphus – he was the man that pushed the stone, pushed up the stone –

Mr. B: *Only to have it come down.*

Mr. M: – and have it come down. Well, I –

Mr. B: *Camus wrote, "Il faut supposer Sisyphus heueux."*

Mr. M: Fair enough.

Mr. B: *But I once quoted that and was reprimanded by a correspondent who said, "You missed the whole point. Sisyphus was condemned to unhappiness." Now Camus groped with this and came really around, in a sense, to your – in this case, rather hopeful – conclusion –*

Mr. M: Yes.

Mr. B: *"Il faut supposer Sisyphus heureux."*

Mr. M: Yes, but I think this is right. I mean, I think you could roll a stone to the glory of God. You know, there's a beautiful poem of Herbert's about how one of the most happy people is a woman who brushes out a room to the glory of God. That's happiness. Everything can be done even probably poor old Sisyphus' job, recognising it as part of his destiny. Camus was right. We must assume that he was happy doing it.

Mr. B: *Was the Flying Dutchman happy?*

Mr. M: (laughing) It's difficult for me to put myself in that position of the Flying Dutchman. I don't know whether he was happy or not, but there's no reason – I mean, I can imagine a happy Flying Dutchman, you see, depending on his attitude of mind to himself and what he was doing. The pursuit of happiness – why I was suggesting that it had the most devastating consequences is because it presupposes, indeed, I suppose it was meant to, that there are things: "That is happy. To sleep with that girl will make me happy. To have this money and to be able to do this, that, and the other thing, will make me happy. To be able to be eloquent and applauded will make me happy." None of these things make us happy. They are wretched things. But then, there is this extraordinary happiness, and the happiness lies in being aware that, as a human being created by God, one is fulfilling God's purpose, and that therefore, this extraordinary happiness overwhelms one. And that's what I meant by mystical ecstasy. Mystical ecstasy is the awareness of that happiness.

Mr. B; I take it too, then, it is an awareness of the transience of our experience on earth, because in one of your final propositions, you put it this way: "I have never doubted that our existence in this world has some sort of sequel. It would seem to me preposterous to suppose that this universe was set up solely to provide a mise en scène *for the interminable soap opera of history with its stock characters and situations endlessly repeatea." Now, because you think it preposterous, you think there is life everlasting or do you think there is life everlasting because we were told by Christ that there was life everlasting?*

Mr. M: Well, both.

Mr. B: And the knowledge of it shows how preposterous the soap opera of history is?

Mr. M: Absolutely. That's what the Incarnation did.

Mr. B: So you would deduce heaven from the study of this world and deduce the nature of this world from a study of revelation?

Mr. M: I would deduce heaven from all the things in this world – hints, tiny hints of heaven – from all the things in this world that are beautiful and loving and good, you see? And those things all contain hints of heaven, especially, of course, love.

Mr. B: Notwithstanding that, under the aspect of the heavens, they are trivialised?

Mr. M: They are, because realising that they contain hints

of heaven, you realise how miserably and wretchedly inadequate they are. But still the hint is there, you see.

Mr. B: *Divine intimation.*

Mr. M: Yes, that's exactly it. Wordsworth's poem, "Intimations" is exactly the same sort of idea. That's how I see it, and the idea that man's achievements are in themselves superlative: they're only superlative because they contain that hint. Take away that, and they're nothing. Nothing at all. And that's why when people haven't got that, they tend to build a building that goes miles and miles into the sky, thinking, "If only I can make it as high as that, it will be the wonder of the world." It won't be the wonder of the world because it doesn't contain that special hint of what heaven is like. Time contains hints of eternity, and it's only through those hints of eternity in time that we can bear time.

Mr. B: *Otherwise, time would be endless.*

Mr. M: Time would be endless and unbearable.

Mr. B: *Finally, you frame what you call the most important happening in the world. "It is," you say, "the resurgence of Christianity in the Soviet Union, demonstrating that the whole mighty effort sustained over sixty years to brainwash the Russian people into accepting materialism has been a fiasco. In the long run, governments, however powerful, fall flat on their faces before The Word, which two thousand years ago came to dwell among us full of grace and truth. In other words, absolute power collapses when confronted with absolute love." You deduce or do not deduce from this extremely hopeful phenomenon, i.e. the failure with all the mechanisms of modern totalitarianism to extirpate Christianity from Russia, that the Soviet regime is doomed to fall on its face — to fail?*

Mr. M: Well, every –

Mr. B: It's failed already.

Mr. M: Yes, completely failed, because it has not succeeded in producing human beings on its terms.

Mr. B: The Marxist man.

Mr. M: Yes, that's right. It hasn't come about and never could anybody have had a better opportunity. Of course, it made this enormous impression on me because I would have considered it absolutely inconveivable in Russia –

Mr. B: Fifty years ago.

Mr. M: – in the early thirties when I was there and saw that every single thing anybody read, everything they heard, everything they were taught at school, every conceivable hint that there would be anything else except man, and anything else except man exerting power to create perfect circumstances for himself, that despite that – the refusal to allow anything else – this extraordinary survival of the opposite proposition spread, not through the agencies of propaganda, but through the Gulag Archipelago.

Mr. B: From which you deduce that it is something that resides in the human spirit that cannot possibly be extinguished?

Mr. M: Exactly. Nothing can extinguish it. Till the end of time it shall be there, and it will always manifest itself. And men must never lose heart because of that. That's the reason they must never, not because they think, "If we can just rearrange our currency, we'd get a better gross national product," or "We could invent some source of energy that would be inexhaustible." All the difficult ideas that they have are absolutely worthless. The great guarantee that human life is always worth creating, always worth bringing into this world, always worth living, is because there is built into it this indestructible awareness that it belongs to eternity and not to time.

Mr. B: Then the worldly challenge is to struggle for a society that permits the fertilisation of that instinct.

Mr. M: Yes, but the funny thing is, you see, that the societies in which the fertilisation has been permitted are the ones that are –

Mr. B: About to commit suicide.

Mr. M: Yes, and that where it seems to be shining with an incredible brightness is the one place in the world where you wouldn't, under any circumstances, expect to find it surviving.

Mr. B: The Catacombs. Thank you, Malcolm Muggeridge.

This is a transcript of the "Firing Line" programme taped in Sussex, England on February 19, 1983 and telecast later by PBS, in which the interviewer is William F. Buckley, Jr.

Peace and Power

MR. BUCKLEY: In the relatively long history of this programme, entering its nineteenth year, only one guest has appeared seven times, and he is Malcolm Muggeridge. One programme, in which he explored the search of faith, is regularly shown in Christmas week. I hope it is shown well after I am departed, perhaps even after he has departed. He had for many years spoken of himself as an old man, which at eighty-two he technically is. When reminded that at age ninety Harold MacMillan was made an earl, Mr. Muggeridge responded that now he knew for sure that he had nothing to live for.

After almost four years we are back in the home of Mr and Mrs Muggeridge in Sussex. The last programme done here inquired first into the search for faith, and in the second hour, to the question of denominationalism. He asked, in fact, that we call the hour, "Why I am not a Catholic." Twenty-six months after the programme was shown, he and his wife went to a neighbouring church and were baptised. He was asked why by a press always fascinated by their most distinguished living alumnus, and he spoke of, I quote, "a sense of homecoming, of picking up the threads of a lost life, of responding to a bell that has long been ringing, of finding a place at a table that has long been left vacant." I suppose we should touch on what it was that he now heard in the tone of that bell, before moving on to explore a relatively recent phenomenon, namely the rise of Christian pacifism: particularly, or so it would seem sometimes in America, within the Catholic Church.

So: I begin by asking the question directly. What, Mr Muggeridge, did you now hear in the tintinnabulations of the bells?

MR. MUGGERIDGE: Instead of the bell sounding as something that I couldn't respond to, now I hear it with joy because it means that I go to Mass, and this has been, in old age, a wonderfully fulfilling thing. I think it's just partly good fortune because the little chapel in which we were received, and where we now go is packed with children, and I love to have Mass with all these little children around, and come away feeling enormously happy.

Mr. B: *Well, but why was it that this could not have been anticipated earlier? I ask this question not to tease you, but out of a genuine curiosity. You said four years ago that you were afraid of entering into any discipline in which you would find yourself instantly in the role of a critic more so even than a communicant. What was it that altered that criterion?*

Mr. M: It is because of the experience itself, Bill. That is all I can say, is that it's one of the things in my life. Worship is a beautiful thing and a thing that I missed for many years, and now I enjoy it very much. This morning, for instance, well, thinking of you, as a matter of fact, and of this, Kitty and I went off to Mass, and obviously it is this ancient ritual. I read somewhere in a book recently, which perhaps shed a little bit of light on it, that since the Last Supper, an hour has never passed in which there is not someone in the world receiving – giving and receiving – the sacrament, and it's an amazing thought, that. All the terrible things that have happened and the confusion, and yet this is something that has gone on and on, and now I can participate in it.

Mr. B: *Well, you mentioned in our discussion last time around a second point, namely that the resurgence of faith behind the Iron Curtain reminded one of the special stimulus of catacomb life. Do you reiterate that, now that you still live on the correct side of the Iron Curtain and have an opportunity to worship and receive the sacraments? Do you feel that you are missing something, for instance, that the Pole has got, or the Ukranian Christian or the Czechoslovak?*

Mr. M: I don't think so, no, although what I said then has been only strengthened in what I've heard and read and, in a very limited way, experienced that, strangely enough, the Christian religion is disintegrating in the Western world, without any question, but that it is, in some mysterious manner, growing in power and influence where you would perhaps least expect it, which is in these labour camps. In a conversation that I had with Solzhenitsyn recently, who, of course, is very well versed in what goes on in the Gulag, he makes this point very strongly. In abolishing the Christian faith, the regime has really restored it and that where this suffering takes place, where people are utterly cut off from everything that would normally be thought of as making life worth living, there this amazing hope is reborn.

Mr. B: *Well, there is, of course, a temptation to find a divine purpose in everything. I think that temptation should presumptively be resisted. But the phenomenon to which you allude tempts one to ask whether we might be in fact heading towards apocalypse. It has struck me that the recognition of the world's end is a cliché in Christian doctrine, and yet it strikes me that as that possibility becomes increasingly vivid, there is a fear of it that is in-*

consistent with that philosophical detachment in which it was accepted two thousand years ago. Does that strike you also?

Mr. M: I think there's a tremendous lot in that. I mean, God knows, the necessary forces and scenario is available for such an ending. It's the first time in human history that men have in their hands the means of bringing the world to an end. I mean, they might think they had –

Mr. B: No, I don't want you to predict it –

Mr. M: No, no, no.

Mr. B: – any more than I would want you to do so.

Mr. M: No, but I don't think that. I think that it is part of this experience of living that you see this potential of an end, but that actually there can't be an end and that the circumstances which would bring the end could also bring about the beginning. In other words, putting it in very simple terms, imagine that we do have the lunacy of a great atomic explosion, a nuclear explosion. All right, enormous destruction will take place and enormous numbers of deaths will occur, but also, somewhere or other, somebody will just suddenly be prostrating themselves before some coloured stone or something and it all begins again.

Mr. B: Yes, as that hack Russian writer once wrote, that when all the world is paved in concrete, somewhere a blade of grass will come through. However, let's look at it a bit more totally, if you don't mind –

Mr. M: Please.

Mr. B: – on the understanding that this is an abstract exercise. Carl Sagan, the American scientist, has recently popularised, if that's the right word, the intuition that in fact if three thousand whatever – megabytes or unmegabytes or kilobytes or whatever – go off, it will cause a cosmic winter, which will make survival absolutely impossible. When he told me this, I gave perhaps the wrong reply. Spastically, I said, "Well that's very good news because I should think that would be the ultimate deterrent to that kind of trigger being pressed." But in any case, you began by saying, and I think it's correct, that technically the means do exist to blot out life, including the blade of grass. Now, why should we resist, as our churchmen seem to have done, an attempt to integrate that hypothetical contingency in Christian doctrine?

Mr. M: Well, largely for one reason and one reason alone, which, to me, is absolutely decisive, and that is that ultimately the only prayer there is to say is, "Thy will be done." In other words, if something can happen and if that something happens, it can only be part of the purpose of our Creator for His creation, and that it might seem to be utterly destructive and hopeless, but out of it would come continuation, and this is – even if the whole thing were to be obliterated, still that would be God's purpose. Otherwise, it couldn't happen.

Mr. B: Well, here wouldn't a theologian insist that God's purpose be defined as giving to man the will which can mischievously be exerted to the end of suicide?

Mr. M: Yes.

Mr. B: All right. If somebody commits suicide, it's not God's purpose that he should commit suicide, is it?

Mr. M: No, no, but the fact that it happens means that God willed it to happen.

Mr. B: God willed that we have the power to have it happen?

Mr. M: Yes.

Mr. B: Yes.

Mr. M: And if we had that power, He also willed that in certain circumstances, we might use that power, and a resultant situation would be, in that sense, what He conceives should be brought about.

Mr. B: But the proximate pressure would be the devil's rather than God's, would it not?

Mr. M: The pressure might be the devil's and, to some extent, will be the devil's, but, you see, even the devil's purposes are ultimately turned into God's purpose. It was the devil's purpose that our Lord should be crucified, but in His Crucifixion lay everything that's wonderful in a civilisation that you and I belong to. If that is now going to destroy itself, it can only destroy itself with, not necessarily with God's approval, but with God's consent; and therefore, out of it will come something which is impossible to foresee. Some life far away or some life in the wreckage will suddenly manifest itself, and the whole process will begin.

Mr. B: A transmutation of life into something different?

Mr. M: Yes, could be.

Mr. B: Okay. Well now, let's focus on the phenomenon of the end of the world and ask whether it has had an unhealthy bearing on a number of priests and theologians of every Christian denomination who seem to be approaching Christian pacifism, which was never a traditional position in Christianity. Do you find that the bishop's statement, for instance, in America that made so many headlines a year or so ago, that that sometimes had a taste of idolatry for life in this world in the sense that it was given a priority which it was never intended to have?

Mr. M: Well, I think that is so. There is a lack of humility in quarters where there should be no lack of humility. It's saying that this is the most appalling thing and if this happens, then everything is lost. But everything can't be lost because we are part of the Creation and what happens to us is in some degree, in some particular, the fulfilling of God's purpose for His Creation, and I think that these bishops have been infected with what is the great sickness of the twentieth century, which is science. They've caught that illness, and a lot of the things that they've done which are distressing if you look into them is because they've caught that illness, or this idiotic thing of evolution, which I'm sure will amuse mankind or whoever succeeds mankind for centuries to come – this idea that, you know, there was an amoebic mess and this amoebic mess became Bertrand Russell or somebody like that.

Mr. B: I can believe that.

Mr. M: (laughing) Yes. That this is a sort of craziness that science has fed into life, and produced an inanity which no previous supposition has. The hierarchy are disgracing themselves quite often by falling into that trap.

Mr. B: Well, as I understand it, here is the distinction that they attempt to make. It is correct that Christianity has never adopted pacifism, certainly not the Catholic Church. It has accepted the notion that some things are worth dying for, in pursuit of. Not suicide, but in pursuit of, let's say, of safety for your family, you may venture out and expose yourself to the possibility of death. Now, what's different now, say many of them, is that the corporate decision, of which I gave a particular example, is one that holds hostage the survival of the human race, and that the stakes, therefore, are too great to justify going out to protect the safety of the hearth, which means going out with hydrogen bombs and perhaps this three hundred megatons or whatever it is that's sufficient to destroy the earth; this, they say, is a quantum jump away from the conventional understanding of Christian hierarchy, and for that reason, some of them are finding themselves uttering pacifist pieties, which really call for unilateral surrender. Now, do you see anything in the fact of the bomb that invalidates preceding thinking as it touches on Christian pacifism?

Mr. M; No, I don't. You see, I think that part of the fallacy of their position is seeing this bomb as a unique threat.

Mr. B: Why is that a fallacy?

Mr. M: Well, because it's not a unique threat. I mean, because mankind has been under attack in various ways throughout his history. In the Latin Council in the twelfth century, a resolution was taken that the crossbow was such an evil, monstrous weapon that no Christian should use it. It could, however, be used against heathens, but not against Christians, this diabolical weapon. Multiply that by a billion billion billion, and you have the atomic bomb.

Mr. B: But do you? You see, they say that's not true. They say you're using a synecdoche when you talk about one man with a crossbow; but, say they, when the target is life itself, you've got to usher in more sophisticated rules. Now, I'm anxious to hear your analysis of why that isn't so.

Mr. M: Well, it isn't so because in fact it's not a difference in kind; it's a difference in degree. You see, for instance, because my memory goes back a long way now, and in all the prognostications about the '39–'45 war were that "the airplanes will always get through, saturation bombing will take place, we're all going to be destroyed." In fact, they, as human beings always do, produced some very bizarre ideas. One was that there should be an enormous store of coffins available – and this sounds as though I'm making it up, but I'm not – and there wasn't enough wood for all the coffins that would be required by this holocaust, so they had cardboard coffins.

Mr. B: *But they were more nearly right than wrong, weren't they? The deaths in World War I were fifteen million. In the Second World War, fifty-five million, leading up to Hiroshima. So wouldn't you say that there was a certain amount of prophetic validity in what they –*

Mr. M: Not really, because I think that it presupposes that this miserable, ridiculous, little creature, *homo sapiens,* will be able totally to destroy God's creation, and he won't. That's all. I mean, Hiroshima, again, is a very good example. It so happened that I went there very soon after the end of the war in a train with the emperor because General MacArthur told the emperor that he wasn't a sun god any more; he was an ordinary king and he must wear a hat and raise it and so on.

Mr. B: *He was just a dumpy, frumpy and banal king?*

Mr. M: Absolutely. Well, then we got to Hiroshima, this place of doom. But of course it wasn't a place of doom. And you know, the only man I ever met who actually lived through the bomb in Hiroshima was the late head of the Jesuits, Arrupe.

Mr. B: *He was there?*

Mr. M: He was a priest there.

Mr. B: I didn't know that.

Mr. M: And I asked him about all these things, a sort of black rain and all these things that were built up in the picture, you know, in that single issue of *The New Yorker* –

Mr. B: Yes, John Hersey's.

Mr. M: – that brought it all out. And of course, it was a very, very bad explosion, a very destructive explosion.

Mr. B: Mr Muggeridge, I don't – you don't intend to communicate – or do you? – that we are exaggerating the apocalyptic powers of the existing inventory of weapons. If whoever it was who counted is correct, we have six-hundred million times the explosive power of the Hiroshima bomb in our current inventory.

Mr. M: Yes. Bill, I don't take those figures. I mean, they are true, but the implications of them are not true. If there is a nuclear bomb, a nuclear explosion that destroys everything, if there's one single black man in the middle of some huge jungle still alive, then it hasn't destroyed mankind. It'll begin again. It'll go on. I mean, it's the idea that this thing we've got will in fact obliterate the human race, and that, too, again, is only obliterating the occupants of one very small, little feature in the universe, and to regard that as the end of everything is the mad ego that develops.

Mr. B: Well, it may be just a little acre, but it's our planet's little acre, isn't it?

Mr. M: It is our planet, and I'm very fond of it in a way.

Mr. B: You seem to resist, for reasons that aren't plain

to me yet, the notion that in fact it is written that the end of the world will come.

Mr. M: It could come. I doubt if it could come in human terms. I don't think that it could come in God's terms because the whole idea is built not upon God's purposes, but upon man's purpose; and man's purpose is always wrong.

Mr. B: Well, it was certainly wrong in crucifying Him, but in fact, people seem to be arguing, even people whose roots are in Christian thought, that although the New Testament does speak about the end of the world, such a thing is really inconceivable, and that, under the circumstances, all policy should be written around preventing that possibility and that the shrewdest way to do that is to destroy, even unilaterally, our nuclear inventory, which, to me, is lunatic and heretical in its implications. But I don't want to argue with them that they may in fact be right that the next time around not even one black man in Africa will survive, or one blade of grass.

Mr. M: Well, of course, we can't really decide, you know, exactly what's going to happen, but there is an element of scientific egotism, and pride built into the idea that having invented this thing, life's over, if used. This is absolutely typical madness of the scientific mind. I don't think that is at all what the end of the world, as envisioned by people like the Apostle Paul, was.

Mr. B: What did he have in mind?

Mr. M: What he had in mind was the coming again of our Lord. That was the essential thing, and that would be more important and more sublime than anything that human beings could do. I mean, that was what the end of the world was – the end of the reign of man and that

Christ would come again and life would be quite different. Now, this is a dream, but it's a very beautiful dream, and I don't think that it can be equated in any way with the use of an ultrapowerful nuclear bomb, which would, of course, do enormous damage. The other day the Pope said something. He's a good man, that Pope, and he now and again says terribly good things. And he said the trouble with this nuclear thing is not really the bomb; the trouble is that there should be men who would use the bomb; that's the terrible thing, and that's the devil's thing. I quite agree. I think he's absolutely right.

Mr. B: Well, I think he's absolutely right, and I think he's correct that people forget that. James Burnham pointed out years ago in his seminal book that a rifle is no more deadly that a broomstick in the absence of the will to use it as a rifle. But we do know that there are people alive who would not cavil at the use of the bomb if in fact it could be guaranteed to bring about what it was that they sought to bring about. Now, is there in the net dialectical situation an argument for throwing away our atom bombs? On the Christian principle?

Mr. M: I don't think at this moment that there is. There could be. There could come a time when it might seem right to do it, but now I think that the one hope of preventing this, not apocalypse, but the total destruction of everything we call Western Civilisation is this. Let me go to a sort of frightfully small point really. I happened to be in America when the Cuban crisis was going on, and there was Khrushchev and John F. Kennedy meeting together, and you could see exactly that each of them was thinking, you know, "Well, he's got this and we don't want him to have it." In other words, they didn't want a nuclear war and there wasn't a nuclear war. And you could have of course, a situation in which the person who's Khrushchev does want it because he thinks that, owing to all this peace business that is being stirred up, that a decisive victory could be won by the Communist powers. That is possibly true. But I don't think that if you have two relatively equal nuclear force potentials, that is a situation which is not terribly dangerous. It becomes dangerous if one of them becomes so weak that the temptation to the other to use its superiority would be to use it over there.

Mr. B: Is that the imaginary situation in which you said you might make the point that Christian duty prescribed throwing away your nuclear arsenal?

Mr. M: I didn't think that it implies that.

Mr. B: Well, what did you have in mind when you said under some circumstances that might be –

Mr. M: Well, it might be the case that –

Mr. B: – recommended.

Mr. M: It might be the case that there could be an agreement, a real agreement, not a faked agreement, but a real agreement, to get rid of this in exactly the same way that at a much lower level the danger of poison gas, the danger of bacteriological war –

Mr. B: Yes, but that's not unilateral, if there's an agreement, is there?

Mr. M: No, it's not, but it is –

Mr. B: So you're not really anxious to specify a circumstantial situation in which you would recommend, as a Christian, that we unilaterally do away with –

Mr. M: In the present set up of the world, no. I think

that it's absolutely a foolish notion, which has been largely stimulated by people who want to make sure that the East is the strong side, and those people are working away like beavers. We have a local Monsignor here who lends himself to this. It's one of the few changes that take place, because before it was the Dean of Canterbury, an Anglican, but now we have a Monsignor who says that the Communists, for instance, are men of peace.

Mr. B: Sort of like the Red dean twenty-five years ago, Hewlett Johnson.

Mr. M: That's right, he reappears as a Monsignor.

Mr. B: Well, I suppose to say you're a man of peace in the generic sense is not to commit an empirical error, but if you point at Stalin and say, "This was a man of peace," it's extremely difficult to carry the metaphor, isn't it?

Mr. M: Bill, there is a peace, and funnily enough, in meditating on all this business, it came to me rather vividly because a rather strange thing happened. When we were trying to get the Nobel peace prize for Mother Teresa, which we had to do several years in succession to get, and then she finally got it, and the question came back from Oslo, which is where the thing is settled by these rather sombre Norwegian senators who decide who is the person of peace, that – the question came back, "What does Mother Teresa do for peace?" In other words, where does she sort of march and recite slogans and hold hands around missile sites and so on and so on; what has she done for peace?

Mr. B: That's right, right.

Mr. M: I mean, those two great forces in our existence of power and love. She is the one who lives in terms of love. Now, that is really working for peace. That is really overcoming the menace of people who are going to totally destroy our world and ourselves. But it struck me as very humorous in a way that somebody should want to be given some point in her activities which you could say, "That is definitely in the direction of peace," and I suppose, for the people who put that question, if she had actually joined this so-called peace movement that would have met the case. But of course it's much more than that.

Mr. B: *Yes.*

Mr. M: In her, one can see why the Christian can confront the danger of a nuclear holocaust without undue fear.

Mr. B: *Well, surely in the case of Mother Teresa you have an example of somebody who is carrying out so explicitly the injunction that she should love her neighbours as to entitle you to say, "If everybody loved their neighbours as she loves her neighbours, you would not crank up the kind of hostility that would bring on belligerence."*

Mr. M: Exactly.

Mr. B: *Well, do you acknowledge or not the following line of reasoning, namely that if in a nuclear exchange, the victim of the first strike, in this case, the West, were to proceed to fire back, although it's too late, according to my accounting, to prevent that first strike, you don't necessarily repeal the doctrine of deterrence because you have accomplished something in virtue of firing back and ridding the world of such aggressors as committed the first strike. Do you have a moral justification, in other words, in firing back with the sole purpose of ridding the world of such aggressors? That's the question.*

Mr. M: Yes, well, I think that it's a matter which I

couldn't in advance say.

Mr. B: But you would have to if you were president, wouldn't you?

Mr. M: Yes, you would have to envisage the possibility of that.

Mr. B: We intend to run you, you know.

Mr. M: Yes, you would have to do that, and it's certainly very important that the people who are going to send the first shot know quite well – that this one is coming back because that is the best of all deterrents –

Mr. B: Right, right, right. And in the absence of that certitude there's an attrition of the deterrent factor.

Mr. M: It increases enormously the danger of the thing being precipitated from one quarter. That is indeed true.

Mr. B: Yes.

Mr. M: And so that pacifism in the sense of saying that, "We will get rid of all our weapons," well, yes, if you are prepared to have no authority in the world, no influence in the world, no importance in the world; to wind up your role as a country, as a people. That is one sort of pacifism, and it's one that I couldn't bring myself to respect. But the idea that you would give up your nuclear weapons and then whoever gets over his illness and can function in the Kremlin would then say, "Well, it's not much good us having nuclear weapons if these people have given them up," that is pure drivel, isn't it?

Mr. B: Yes, C.S. Lewis said that the pacifists have a vested interest in losing their campaign.

Mr. M: Yes.

Mr. B: Because the belligerents would not permit them to be pacifists, and under the circumstances, they can only continue to be pacifists for so long as they lose the popular campaign. Pacifists are not tolerated in the Soviet Union. Under the circumstances, the sure way to guarantee that you would end your pacifist existence would be to surrender to the Soviet Union. So although that point sometimes sounds a little too trim and neat, I think it is a profoundly interesting point.

Mr. M: So do I.

Mr. B: Now, when you speak of the disintegration of Christian life, do you mean exclusively among the laity or also among the clergy?

Mr. M; Well, I mean both, actually.

Mr. B: So is there not visible a resistance to that disintegration among the organised clergy?

Mr. M: I suspect there might be. I haven't actually come across it myself, but I suspect there might be because the clergy are subject to the fantasies of human beings, and that's one.

Mr. B: I know a scholar who a year or so ago said, "You know, I've been dying to become a Catholic for about ten to twelve years, but I can't get anybody interested enough to tell me about it," and I thought that was extremely interesting.

Mr. M: Very interesting, yes.

Mr. B: The notion that religious evangelism should have

a very low social priority, is really quite new, or is it? Is that a twentieth century phenomenon?

Mr. M: I'm not quite sure what you mean by that.

Mr. B: Well, in most centuries people had what they called "fighting faiths," and although they were often stupid about how they attempted to evangelise, the Inquisition being a notorious example, still they cared. And the question arises whether in the twentieth century people care enough to bother, for instance, to preach the word of Christ, even at the risk of being boring. Is that a part of the disintegration that you isolate? That lack of zest?

Mr. M: I would think it probably is, but I still am not quite sort of clear myself as to exactly what's in their minds over that. I think that it could be regarded as a sort of deterioration, as a loss of faith, in a way. I feel the ultimate faith of the Christian religion is that God is responsible for Creation, and God is a God of love, not of hate; God is all the qualities that we want to see in the world, and that nothing can be settled except in relation to that. Man can make an inconceivable mess of anything, and I would say that he's putting up a tremendous performance at this moment, partly by this utter acceptance of the idea that this bomb makes nothing worthwhile.

Mr. B: Well, when we pray that we be delivered from temptation, might it be correct to say that a temptation in having a nuclear arsenal is to use it, even if your motives are defensive rather than aggressive, and that under the circumstances, it is prudent to remove such a temptation from yourself, yourself, of course, being a country?

Mr. M: That would be quite a good idea provided the people who put it forward will recognise exactly what that would mean. If they would get rid of all their weapons, they would then count for absolutely nothing in the world. They would be of no importance whatever. They would have no influence whatever upon what happens. After all, there are countries that have reached that point, small countries like Scandinavian countries who haven't really got any defences, and who seem to get along all right for the time being. I think that the notion that we must get rid of all these weapons at all costs, and that if we do we shall live happily ever after, is a great fantasy, and one that is planted on us to some extent by pressures that are really quite different but don't admit to being so.

Mr. B: *Now, those pressures. Do they emanate from people who simply are unrealistic, or do they emanate from people who are sentimental about the Soviet Union? Somebody said about you that the only sense in which you have been feveredly consistent is your opposition to Communism ever since you discovered it in Moscow in 1932. Is this consistency of opposition to Communism by you something that derives from a special knowledge of Communism, or is it generally communicable among people who haven't had your experience?*

Mr. M: Well, obviously it exists because of that experience, which, for me, was a great sort of turnover of views about life, and it was intensified by this spectacle, which I still think is one of the strangest of all that one's experienced, which is the spectacle of the choice intelligentsia of the Western world prostrating themselves before Stalin and his setup there.

M.r B: *And how do you account for that?*

Mr. M: I can't yet. I mean, of course there are different features of it, but I think that a lot of the people who went there and some who were known to me, even related through marriage, that what they wanted to feel was that they could have power, absolute power, without going through all the rigamarole of being elected and making their views acceptable.

Mr. B: But why did they want the power?

Mr. M: Because they love power. Because people who have not realised that the basis of human life is love, do love power and pine for power.

Mr. B: Well, do they in some cases pine for power because they feel that they can genuinely make a better world through the exercise of it?

Mr. M: They persuade themselves of that.

Mr. B: Yes.

Mr. M: It's rather like someone attempting a seduction and saying that, "After all, this will do you good," you know. I mean, they are absolutely avid for power for power's own sake. This is something that's in human beings, and it is enormously evident in ideologies, and they may see this setup in the USSR and where, you know, everything can be done because you are completely free to do what seems to you right.

Mr. B: Basically the urge for power is a very dangerous one. It's one that Jesus Christ declined to have.

Mr. M: Yes, but certainly if you were, let's say, being tormented by Hitler in the '30s, you would welcome power sufficient to resist, wouldn't you?

Mr. B: That's what a war's about, isn't it?

Mr. M: Yes. But you're, let's say, a contender. A political

contender for office in 1932 would desire power perhaps for the best of reasons. He would think they were the best of reasons.

Mr. B: But it would corrupt?

Mr. M: Yes, and it would also be something that appealed to him. In other words, instead of having to argue with a lot of difficult people and address a lot of meetings and things, he would be in a position to do what he thought was the right thing on his own strength. At least that was the only explanation I could see for all these extraordinary people coming there because everything in the regime and in the way in which it operated was contrary to what they believed in and liked. But it still had the marvellous point in its favour that it gave you absolute power. I mention a very small example. We were taken down to the Dneprostroi Dam when it finished, and there was an American colonel who had been building it, and I asked him, purely as sort of conversation, "How do you like it here?" expecting some marvellous tirade, and he said, "Oh it's absolutely superb." And so I said, "Why do you think it's superb?" And he said, "Well, because, you see, we never have any labour troubles." And that seems to me to embody the whole thing. I mean, from his view, it was perfect. You were building a dam, you wanted a thousand more people, telephone to the GPU and they come, no questions asked, no pay discussions.

Mr. B: What Michael Oakeshott calls "making politics as the crow flies."

Mr. M: Yes.

Mr. B: Well, but the scholastic Christian philosophy teaches us that government is a divine institution. What do you understand to be meant by that assertion?

Mr. M: I've never met a government that seemed to me to be a divine institution, I'm afraid. But it is true that power has to be exercised, which is presumably what Jesus Christ meant when he said, "We render unto Caesar the things that are Caesar's and unto God, the things that are God's."

Mr. B: So therefore there are some things that should be Caesar's?

Mr. M: Exactly.

Mr. B: For instance, a police force, right?

Mr. M: Yes. They're all dangerous, even then, but they're also necessary. But in answering that question about "Should we pay tribute to Caesar?" He does recognise that Caesar has claims upon us. If we enjoy the security –

Mr. B: That he gives you.

Mr. M: That he gives us.

Mr. B: Yes, and that would translate nowadays, for instance, in the right to conscript –

Mr. M: Yes.

Mr. B: – an army in England or in America.

Mr. M: To limit what's called freedom under certain circumstances.

Mr. B: Yes, yes. But the quest for power in democratic circumstances, you are saying, is self-governing; that is to say, you run less of a risk of accumulating as much of it as you would if you didn't have the democratic tribunal to pass judgement. Well, let me then finish in the last five minutes we have by asking you to sum up on this point. Is there anything that's happened in your lifetime which you think affects those priorities on the basis of which Christianity for two thousand years has told us that there is such a thing as a just war?

Mr. M: I think that is a question that I have a great difficulty in giving a sort of "yes" and "no" answer to, but in one's personal life, in 1939 it seemed to me right that we should fight Hitler, that, if we were to abandon Europe to Hitler, this would be an appalling thing. Afterwards, when it turned out that in fact by knocking off Hitler we simply abandoned ourselves to Stalin, I felt less enthusiastic about it. But it is true that there is such a thing as a just war. There are circumstances in which, if you are going to maintain your civilised way of life, you may have to defend it, and if not, all you can do is to say that, "I'm not prepared to defend it, I don't think that these weapons and things should be used, and therefore I recognise that I must give up every idea of being secure in my way of life and being looked after in any way."

Mr. B: As you may or may not know, there is a protocol in gambling houses, and that protocol is that you may not be given credit. Now, some people do anyway. The idea there is that you should put up only as many chips as you can actually commandeer through the exercise of your financial resources, because otherwise you end up gambling your house and your children's education money or whatever. Now, in a sense, that's something that invokes proportionality. There are people, Christian theologians, who are saying that the proportionality that governed the idea of the just war is now out of bounds, that the kind of credit, the chips, which you were given up until the discovery of the nuclear bomb were realisable, whereas you now have a dimension that would be the equivalent of total credit. You don't believe, for instance, in your right to gamble your own soul, or do you?

Mr. M: It's a very good image, actually of the whole thing. I see the difficulty.

Mr. B: But you're not pronouncing on it?

Mr. M: I'm pronouncing on it in this sense, that if a person is ready to say that, "Because this bomb and a nuclear war would be so terrible, I herewith give up all idea of securing my property, my family, of looking after anything. I give it up because it seems to me that the price to be paid, if it's nuclear war, is too great."

Mr. B: You as an individual or you as a corporate state?

Mr. M: Well, first of all as an individual.

Mr. B: Yes, yes.

Mr. M: And then insofar as you influence the state, yes, also as a state.

Mr. B: We call this Finlandisation in America.

Mr. M: Yes, but even that's a cheat because the Finns are not quite, utterly in the hands of the Communists.

Mr. B: But that's by sufferance of the Communists, isn't it?

Mr. M: Well, it is in a way, but they're also rather cunning themselves. I mean, I think that the Russians use it, of course. They have let it be like that, which doesn't matter to them one way or the other, in order that they can use that argument.

Mr. B: *Sure, it's like China letting Hong Kong be as it is.*

Mr. M: That's right, that's right.

Mr. B: *But it is by sufferance. Now, if one were offered by some divine arbiter the exchange of life as it is lived in Finland, i.e., with as many freedoms as they have and none other, one might say. "Well, this is better than risking a nuclear exchange." On the other hand, there would be no guarantee, would there, that they would be able to –*

Mr. M: No, and this is exactly what's happening actually. The next move in this game, unless there is trouble inside the USSR, is that the West Germans will say that, "After all, we've had a sort of Finland settlement," and call it a day, in which case the triumph of the Communist setup will be total, and probably the United Kingdom and the other small countries will be forced to fall into the same thing.

Mr. B: *Sure. They always talk about what if the Soviet Union said to West Germany, "Pull out of NATO and disband your army, and we will allow you to unify with East Germany and you will have one Germany," which might look wonderful on Monday, but what happens on Tuesday is what we need to remind them, isn't it?*

Mr. M: It's been a very clever move of the Communists to sit up and say, "Well, look at these people. They're quite happy, and so on." You see?

Mr. B: *Yes. "What's so bad about Finlandisation?"*

Mr. M: Exactly. Actually, we had a team here to ask about Orwell and – frightfully nice people – and I said to them, "Supposing I say that Orwell's account of things in *1984* and *Animal Farm* is based entirely on the arrangements in the Soviet Union. Would you allow that to be spoken?" And he said, "I'm afraid not."

Mr. B: *Thank you very much, Mr Malcolm Muggeridge.*

Mr. M: Thank you.